T0193817

Social Informatics Evolving

Synthesis Lectures on Information Concepts, Retrieval, and Services

Editor
Gary Marchionini, *University of North Carolina, Chapel Hill*

Synthesis Lectures on Information Concepts, Retrieval, and Services publishes short books on topics pertaining to information science and applications of technology to information discovery, production, distribution, and management. Potential topics include: data models, indexing theory and algorithms, classification, information architecture, information economics, privacy and identity, scholarly communication, bibliometrics and webometrics, personal information management, human information behavior, digital libraries, archives and preservation, cultural informatics, information retrieval evaluation, data fusion, relevance feedback, recommendation systems, question answering, natural language processing for retrieval, text summarization, multimedia retrieval, multilingual retrieval, and exploratory search.

© Springer Nature Switzerland AG 2022

Reprint of original edition © Morgan & Claypool 2015

All rights reserved. No part of this publication may be reproduced, stored in a retrieval system, or transmitted in any form or by any means—electronic, mechanical, photocopy, recording, or any other except for brief quotations in printed reviews, without the prior permission of the publisher.

Social Informatics Evolving
Pnina Fichman, Madelyn R. Sanfilippo, and Howard Rosenbaum

ISBN: 978-3-031-01169-6   print
ISBN: 978-3-031-02297-5   ebook

DOI 10.1007/978-3-031-02297-5

A Publication in the Springer series
SYNTHESIS LECTURES ON INFORMATION CONCEPTS, RETRIEVAL, AND SERVICES #46
Series Editor: Gary Marchionini, University of North Carolina, Chapel Hill

Series ISSN 1947-945X Print 1947-9468 Electronic

Social Informatics Evolving

Pnina Fichman, Madelyn R. Sanfilippo, and Howard Rosenbaum

Rob Kling Center for Social Informatics, School of Informatics and Computing, Indiana University, Bloomington

SYNTHESIS LECTURES ON INFORMATION CONCEPTS, RETRIEVAL, AND SERVICES #46

ABSTRACT

The study of people, information, and communication technologies and the contexts in which these technologies are designed, implemented, and used has long interested scholars in a wide range of disciplines, including the social study of computing, science and technology studies, the sociology of technology, and management information systems. As ICT use has spread from organizations into the larger world, these devices have become routine information appliances in our social lives, researchers have begun to ask deeper and more profound questions about how our lives have become bound up with technologies. A common theme running through this research is that the relationships among people, technology, and context are dynamic, complex, and critically important to understand. This book explores social informatics (SI), one important and dynamic approach that researchers have used to study these complex relationships. SI is "the interdisciplinary study of the design, uses and consequences of information technology that takes into account their interaction with institutional and cultural contexts" (Kling 1998, p. 52; 1999). SI provides flexible frameworks to explore complex and dynamic socio-technical interactions. As a domain of study related largely by common vocabulary and conclusions, SI critically examines common conceptions of and expectations for technology, by providing contextual evidence.

This book describes the evolution of SI research and identifies challenges and opportunities for future research. In what might be seen as an example of socio-technical "natural selection," SI emerged in six different locations during the 1980s and 1990s: Norway, Slovenia, Japan, the former Soviet Union, the UK and, last, the U.S. As SI evolved, the version popularized in the US became globally dominant. The evolution of SI is presented in five stages: emergence, foundational, expansion, coherence, and transformation. Thus, we divide SI research into five major periods: an emergence stage, when various forms of SI emerged around the globe, an early period of foundational work which grounds SI (Pre-1990s), a period of *expansion* (1990s), a robust period of coherence and influence by Rob Kling (2000–2005),[1] and a period of *transformation* (2006–present).

Following the description of the five periods we discuss the evolution throughout the periods under five sections: principles, concepts, approaches, topics, and findings. *Principles* refer to the overarching motivations and labels employed to describe scholarly work. *Approaches* describe the theories, frameworks, and models employed in analysis, emphasizing the multi-disciplinary and interdisciplinary nature of SI. *Concepts* include specific processes, entities, themes, and elements

---

[1] This time period extends two years after Rob Kling's death because some of his publications appeared later, and many publications that appeared immediately after his death were not only strongly inspired by him but also a tribute to him and his SI research.

of discourse within a given context, revealing a shared SI language surrounding change, complexity, consequences, and social elements of technology. *Topics* label the issues and general domains studied within social informatics, ranging from scholarly communication to online communities to information systems. *Findings* from seminal SI works illustrate growing insights over time and demonstrate how repeatable explanations unify SI. In the concluding remarks, we raise questions about the possible futures of SI research.

KEYWORDS

Social informatics, socio-technical, information and communication technology (ICT), social aspects of technology, ICT use, ICT design

Contents

Acknowledgments

Many thanks to Gary Marchionini (University of North Carolina, Chapel Hill) for his support of this book on Social Informatics. We also greatly appreciate the comments and suggestions provided by Bob Mason (University of Washington), Ken Fleischman (University of Texas, Austin), and Eric Meyer (Oxford Internet Institute) in their reviews. Finally, we are thankful for the support of Diane Cerra from Morgan and Claypool.

CHAPTER 1

Introduction

In this book we describe the current status and possible future directions of social informatics (SI), as well as the origins and development of the discipline. SI is an approach to studying the social aspects of computing that takes into account the complex interplay between information and communication technologies (ICT), the people who design, implement, manage, and use them, and the contexts of their design and use. This book has been developed as a follow up that integrates and expands on Fichman and Rosenbaum's (2014) edited volume *Social Informatics: Past, Present, and Future*. It covers the evolution of SI research, articulates its major principles and approaches as well as its critical concepts, topics, and significant findings, and concludes by identifying challenges and opportunities for future research.

This book has been written for two main audiences: (1) graduate and advanced undergraduate students who can use this book to learn about SI, and (2) scholars who have a curiosity about theoretically rich and empirically grounded approaches to critically examine the taken-for-granted assumptions, beliefs, and discourses that surround ICT, the people who design, implement, manage, and use them, and the wide range of settings in which these activities take place.

Of particular interest to these audiences is the emergence and development of SI, which has paralleled the increasing ubiquity of digital technologies and computerization in our work and social lives. SI, in fact, takes this powerful and fundamental phenomenon as its primary object of study and therefore becomes an important way that we can learn about ourselves and our complex relationships with the technologies we use all day, every day. We hope that reading and thinking about the evolution of SI as explained in this book will spark creative thinking about the ways in which our interactions with these technologies shape our future. Scholars can continue to refine our understanding of the mutual relationships between ICT, people, groups, organizations, professions, and society while investigating a wide range of settings in which ICTs are designed, implemented, and used. Students who pursue careers working with and designing ICT, or careers involved with ICT policy and regulation, or in social justice issues related to ICT, can do so with a keen critical awareness of impacts of technologies on work and play derived from the best of SI research. In a practical sense, students will also find the concluding bibliography very useful because it provides a comprehensive collection of core SI work as well as work influencing SI from cognate domains.

This book is also useful for scholars and students, who can use this book to explore the history and evolution of SI, learning about the main principles, concepts, methods, and findings that constitute its core body of knowledge, all of which, as will be detailed below, come from hundreds of studies of a wide range of ICTs in an even wider range of settings. Hopefully what is in these pages will resonate, and spark research ideas and directions that will shape the future of SI, advancing it into its fourth decade and beyond.

There are several reasons for students and scholars to read and use this book. One is that it is important to question taken-for-granted assumptions about technologies and the ways in which we design and use them. It is also important to question the popular discourses about technologies, because the ways in which we think and talk about them influences our understandings and uses of them and, equally important, ICTs have been adopted on the basis of inaccurate understandings and unreasonable expectations derived from these discourses. It has been clear from the recent past that uncritically accepted discourse about technology can have negative consequences when it becomes a basis for organizational and public policy. For example, during the late 1990s, the discourse about business process re-engineering (BPR) shaped policies that led to layoffs, and large-scale public failures (Lamb, 1996). BPR was based on a technologically determinist argument that the road to increased performance and productivity in the workplace was paved with ICT. Technological determinism still drives much of the development, design, and implementation of ICT. With an approach based in SI, researchers would question this discourse, uncover its unrealistic assumptions, and be able to intervene in the policy process to mitigate potential negative effects.

A second reason is that SI researchers have, since the earliest days in the 1980s, been keenly aware that the social and organizational settings in which ICTs are embedded cannot be ignored. One of the insights that emerged from early SI work that remains important today is the significance of the context. Researchers wondered why the implementation and use of the same information systems in different organizations led to a diversity of outcomes ranging from great success to utter failure. SI researchers have demonstrated time and again that the organizational and socio-cultural contexts of design and use matter. Understanding the SI approach sensitizes researchers, designers, and managers to the importance of context in ICT design, implementation, and use. In an increasingly global and multicultural environment, SI insights about the importance of context for understanding the complex relationship between ICT and people, groups, and society are not only relevant, but are significant and critical (Fichman and Sanfilippo, 2013).

This insight is even more important today as the very nature of the context undergoes significant change. For example, what are we to make of the "Internet of things?" We have seen in the past that when new technologies are introduced and become popular there are always a range of consequences that bring advantages to some and disadvantages to others. Sometimes these consequences can be predicted; sometimes they are unintentional. This was difficult enough when the technologies were visible and would clearly stand out against the background of the context of design and use; a desktop computer has a footprint, as do laptops, tablets, and smartphones. What happens when computing is so embedded in the environment that the technology becomes invisible? What happens when the technology is the context? What happens when all of our electronic devices are connected to the Internet and are continually generating data about themselves and about us?

Should we believe that this vast data generation and collection process is benign? SI will be useful here because it focuses increasingly on ICT, globalization, and related socio-cultural issues, and in doing so, becomes an intellectual key to understanding our technological past, present, and future.

The SI approach is useful because it embraces the complexity of the relationships between people and ICT in social and organizational contexts. This sensitivity to context helps us understand that, for example, making ICT available to a population is not enough to bring about change, particularly in the sense of social justice—there are issues of access, education, and training that also must be taken into account. As well, SI reminds us that the implementation of ICT always has moral and ethical implications.

Using ecological metaphors to describe SI as an evolutionary phenomenon, we show that SI emerged in the academic ecosystem in the 1980s in four different places in the world and again in two more places in the 1990s. Although there was some interaction among the scholars and researchers working in these places, for the most part these versions of SI developed in isolation with the exception of the mid 1990s version in North America, which has arguably become the most dominant version.

The evolution of SI is presented next in five stages: emergence, foundational, expansion, coherence, and transformation. We start with the origins of SI, during the emergence period, describing how it emerged in six different places during the 1980s and 1990s. Then, a discussion of changes in the U.S. version of SI over time, following the next four stages. Five sections will be presented that illustrate how SI has changed, specifically with respect to: (1) principles; (2) concepts; (3) approaches and methods; (4) topics; and (5) findings.

1. **Principles** refer to the overarching motivations and labels employed to describe scholarly work.

2. **Approaches** describe the theories, frameworks, and models employed in analysis, emphasizing the multi-disciplinary and interdisciplinary nature of SI, while methods describe the designs and techniques employed throughout the development of SI.

3. **Concepts** include specific processes, entities, themes, and elements of discourse within a given context, revealing a shared SI language surrounding change, complexity, consequences, and social elements of technology.

4. **Topics** label the issues and general domains studied within SI, ranging from scholarly communication to online communities to information systems.

5. **Findings** from seminal SI works illustrate growing agreement over time and demonstrate how repeatable explanations unify SI.

This part of the book is a valuable review of the SI literature, providing the reader with citations to many of the key works that have shaped SI thinking during these stages in the U.S. In the concluding remarks, we discuss the possible future of SI research.

1.1   SOCIAL INFORMATICS DEFINED

The study of people, ICT, and the contexts in which these technologies are designed, implemented, and used has long interested scholars in a wide range of disciplines, including the social study of computing, science and technology studies, the sociology of technology, and management information systems. As ICT use has spread from organizations into the larger social world, digital devices, from computers to smartphones to game consoles and wearable technologies, have become routine information appliances in our lives and researchers have begun to ask deeper and more profound questions about how our lives have become bound up with these and other technologies. A common theme running through this research is that the relationships among people, technology, and context are dynamic, complex, and critically important to understand. SI is an important and dynamic discipline that focuses squarely on this theme and is an approach within which researchers study these complex relationships from a range of theoretical and methodological perspectives.

SI is "the interdisciplinary study of the design, uses and consequences of information technology that takes into account their interaction with institutional and cultural contexts" (Kling 1998, p. 52). As a community, scholars are united by the SI discipline, based upon common claims about the world and patterns of inquiry that, taken together, form a coherent, yet diverse, tradition. SI provides flexible frameworks for researchers to explore complex and dynamic socio-technical interactions in a range of organizational and social settings. As a domain of study related largely by common vocabulary and conclusions, SI critically examines common conceptions of and expectations for technology, by providing contextual evidence of its meanings and uses.

1.2   EVOLUTIONARY APPROACH TO SOCIAL INFORMATICS

We argue that a valuable way to think about SI is to use evolutionary approaches that are influenced by ecological theories; we are informed by the use of the ecological metaphor in various manifestations at the group (Shachaf and Hara, 2005; Sundstrom et al., 1990), organizational (Adizes, 1979; Hanks et al., 1994), and inter-organizational levels (Doz et al., 2000; Hite and Hesterly, 2001; Ring and Van de Ven, 1994; Shachaf, 2003). Many of these models focus on boundary management. We argue that over time SI has had to face the need to manage its boundaries, despite past efforts to establish boundaries made at specific stages in its development. Successful boundary management is achieved through balancing differentiation and integration. On one hand, SI must differentiate itself from the rest of the scientific and intellectual environment, as a unique approach. Unsuccessful differentiation is a threatening force to SI viability. On the other hand, SI must aim for integration with similar approaches in the external academic environment, because too little integration will result in isolation that eventually may result in its dissolution. These tensions characterize the evolution of SI and their interplay will be an underlying presence as SI moves through the various stages of its development.

A useful framework that we find informative for understanding how SI has evolved over time focuses on the emergence and development of networks (Ring and Van de Ven, 1994; Doz et al., 2000; Hite and Hesterly, 2001). Our approach is also influenced by ecological theories at the individual level, including the social ecological model developed by Bronfenbrenner, as well as principles of development, drawing on biological perspectives (e.g., Wolpert et al., 1998).

Bronfenbrenner, known for his study of human evolution, conceives of evolution and development as a social process and has presented his conceptualization as a framework unifying processes, individuals, context, and time (a process-person-context-time [PPCT] model) (Bronfenbrenner and Morris, 1998), which has lent itself as a model of development to tens of thousands of scholarly works. The social ecological model conceives of context as nested by proximity and strength of influence within multiple levels and represents development as occurring through the production of social knowledge through bidirectional interactions between entities and the environment over time (Bronfenbrenner, 1992). If Bronfenbrenner's model is accepted as indicating why changes occur in development, it can be synthesized with general development stages to explain the origins and changes of a scientific and intellectual discipline, such as SI.

Using a biological perspective, at the level of an individual organism, cells differentiate, embryos develop, and the organism grows, matures, regenerates, and eventually dies (Wolpert et al., 1998). However, at a higher level, such as with species, Darwinian evolution explains the stages of development. Emergence comes from the diversification of past species through natural selection, and as clear differences are established, heredity allows for unifying traits to be passed on and the population develops. With the establishment of a distinct population, variation occurs and over time, this variation leads to diversification and further transformation, though the earlier populations may endure rather than be replaced (Parsons, 1966). Taking this ecological approach to SI we start with the origins of the discipline and describe the competing sources from which SI emerged. Our use of these ecological metaphors throughout this book is limited in an effort to focus on the key concepts, approaches and methods, findings, and topics.

CHAPTER 2

Emergence of Competing Sources of Social Informatics[2]

"In 1996, a small group of researchers interested in the social study of computing agreed that the scattering of related research in a wide array of journals and the use of different nomenclatures was impeding both the research and the abilities of 'research consumers' to find important work. They decided that a common name for the field would be helpful. After significant deliberation, they selected 'social informatics'" (Kling et al., 2005, p. 30).

This section explores the origins and rise of social informatics (SI) by describing the early competing sources from around the globe. As was explained in the Introduction, the ecological approach to the evolution of SI views the discipline as evolving through four stages that are analyzed though the lens of a framework based on principles, concepts, approaches, topics, and findings (Sanfilippo and Fichman, 2014). Prior to the emergent stage, however, scholars and researchers in different parts of the world began to grapple with the complex issues raised by human interactions with ICT. In the later chapters we describe the evolution of SI in the U.S. as the one that arguably is most popular.[3] We will then use a framework that is more of a challenge to apply to the various early ideas because these ideas were nascent, sporadic, and disconnected and were not widely spread beyond those countries where the primary language of publication is not English. However, the framework is useful for the four later stages because it draws attention to "the ways in which social processes and events shape the internal content of intellectual and scientific inquiry" that can lead a movement to "gain control, if only for a limited time, of … the 'intellectual attention space.'" (Frickel and Gross, 2005, p. 204). It also provides a way to understand the evolution of SI in terms of the social and organizational processes through which various forms of SI have emerged, have attempted, with varying degrees of success, to raise their visibility in the global landscape of research on computerization in society, and have sought institutional stability. We start in this section with a description of early ideas that emerged around the globe that formed what we think of SI today, while in the next sections, focusing on the North American version of SI, we provide an in-depth account of the evolution of this version going back in time to its early roots, and continuing through the various stages to the present. First things first; we will start with the basics.

---

[2] A version of this chapter appeared in Fichman, P., and Rosenbaum, H. (eds.) (2014). Chapter 1.
[3] A version of the U.S. development of social informatics research appeared in Fichman, P., and Rosenbaum, H. (eds.) (2014). Chapter 2.

An assumption that underlies what follows is that SI is not simply a literature, or facts and findings about people, ICT, and contexts. Facts and findings and, indeed, SI researchers themselves are embedded in scientific and intellectual communities, educational institutions (typically) and engaged in many routine and taken-for-granted social and organizational practices as they do their work. Given this point of departure, the question can then be asked—how did SI emerge? Did an influential person or group whose presence and activities provided the impetus for the movement to begin bring SI into being? Was it by the publication of an important paper or monograph? Was there a critical incident that marked the origin of SI? Meyer and Rohlinger (2012, p. 145) explain that answering these questions in the affirmative "encourages a fundamental misunderstanding of the process of social change" and ignores the efforts of many individuals and groups, effectively writing them out of the history of a movement. In the case of SI, the process was more complex and nuanced, rooted in particular social, organizational, and historical contexts. As happens in evolution, SI did not suddenly appear as a fully formed intellectual movement at a single moment in time and in a single place; in fact, there were as many as six different versions of SI that gathered themselves together at six different historical moments and in six different locations. Figure 2.1 represents the development of SI over time, illustrating all six distinct points of origin. The first of these was in Norway in the early 1980s and the latest was in the U.S. in the mid 1990s. These versions, over time, have had different trajectories with one of the six, the North American, becoming dominant while others continue locally and sometimes interact with the North American tradition, such as collaborations between British and American SI scholars. Prior to its emergent stage, SI was a collective effort "to pursue research programs or projects for thought in the face of resistance from others in the scientific or intellectual community" (Frickel and Gross, 2005, p. 206). These sources of competition echo Frickel and Gross's (2005, p. 204) insight that

> …the history of almost every field of study … is a history of new scientific or intellectual movements that rose up to challenge established patterns of inquiry, became the subject of controversy, won or failed to win a large number of adherents, and either became institutionalized for a time, until the next movement came along, or faded into oblivion.

In each of the sites where SI emerged, there was an effort to differentiate it in the intellectual landscape by emphasizing two main components: the centrality of the triad of people, ICT, and contexts of design and use and the importance of conceptual frameworks steeped in social science theory. An important outcome of this activity was the development and sharing of a "knowledge core" of SI insights toward which "participants are consciously oriented, regardless of their understanding of it" (Frickel and Gross, 2005, p. 207). The work of establishing this new approach and differentiating it from cognate and competing approaches involved the collective action of scholars and researchers, the recruitment and training of new members, and the development of a shared sense of intellectual identity. Where successful, people involved in these early versions of SI were motivated, to different degrees, to acquire and use resources and raise the SI profile in relevant academic communities through publication, pedagogy, and other professional activities. Taken together, this work was an early and important step in institution building, a necessary development in later SI evolution.

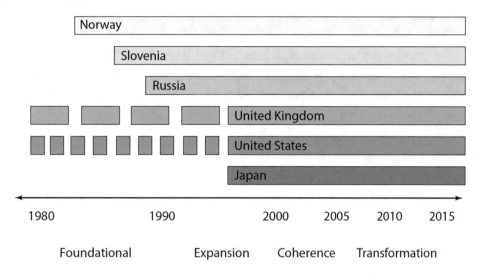

Figure 2.1: A timeline of the development of SI.

The first appearance of SI was in Norway in the early 1980s, where the term was used to describe a research program and domain. Degree-granting academic programs in SI were established in Norwegian and Yugoslavian (later Slovenian) universities in the mid to late 1980s. Around the same time, scholars in the former Soviet Union established an ambitious program in SI research and education. A few years later, in the early 1990s, Japanese scholars began to engage in institution building and publish SI research. At this time in the U.K., several programs and centers devoted to investigating computerization from an SI perspective were established at leading universities. In the mid 1990s, American researchers began to describe studies of the social aspects of computing as SI research; this last version seems to have had the greatest impact in terms of the numbers of publications, conference papers, workshops, and research centers. The ecological framework will be used to illustrate the ways in which various factors helped and hindered the emergence and development of SI in its current form. An important caveat is that the source materials used in this section are published in English, so it is possible that nuances in the development of SI in some of the cultures below may be lost in translation. It may be one of the reasons that the U.S. version of SI had a competitive advantage that fit a wider and obvious niche, which has resulted in a longer lasting impact.

As researchers began to study the effects of computerization in a range of domains various modifiers for the term "informatics" were adopted, such as medical, social, and legal informatics. The earliest use of the modifier "social" was in 1982, when Bråten, a Norwegian social scientist, described the work that he and his colleagues did as "social or socio-informatics" because of its focus on the interrelationships and interdependencies among technology, organizations, and work (Roggen, 2005). Bråten and colleagues established "social informatics [as] the interdisciplinary field of informatics" at the University of Oslo in 1982 (Roggen, 2005). It was originally described as a "scientific domain between psychology, sociology and informatics" (Roggen, 1998) and quickly became the basis of one of the first academic programs in SI when approved by the Norwegian Ministry of Education in 1985 (Vehovar, 2013a).

The second academic program in SI was established in 1985 at the University of Ljubljana, in Yugoslavia (now Slovenia), when the Faculty of Social Sciences began teaching courses that shared a common theme, the "interaction between society and information-communication technologies" at macro and micro levels of analysis (Vehovar, 2013b, The Faculty of Social Sciences, University of Ljubljana, Slovenia; Social Informatics, 2007). In doing so, the Slovenian version of SI anticipated what would become a central theme of later versions, especially that which emerged in the U.S. in the 1990s. Robbin and Day (2006) comment that an outcome of this research and pedagogical activity was that SI was beginning to constitute itself as a discipline.

The third appearance of SI in the intellectual landscape was in the former Soviet Union. According to ISI's Web of Science, the earliest mention (in English) of SI in the academic literature is Ursal's 1989 publication "On the shaping of Social Informatics." Ursal, a philosopher affiliated with the USSR Academy of Science (Vehovar, 2006; p. 76), argues that SI emerged in the Soviet Union because of the extent to which information technologies had become integrated into scientific practice; as a consequence, SI, the study of this phenomenon, was becoming a critically important form of inquiry into the questions raised by the "informatisation" of science, especially social science and, by implication, society. Although not widely known, this is a significant paper because Ursal explores a set of ideas that would become prominent in the version of SI that emerged in the U.S. in the 1990s. SI, he argues (1989, p. 10), should focus on "informatisation," a "socio-technological" process "based on the production and implementation of electronic computing technology." It is a teleological process, the goal of which is to gather "information with the help of informatics means to secure the survival of mankind and a further acceleration of its progress" (Ursal, 1989, p. 10). Also interesting is his use of the concept of mutual shaping to describe the relationship between society and informatics, stating that "informatisation constitutes only one characteristic of the interaction between society and informatics; another is the reciprocal impact of society on informatics development" (1989, p. 10).

The spread of computerization means that as society experiences informatisation, informatics becomes more socialized because computers serve as "a new means of intellectual activity helping to shape a new 'informational' world-outlook and methodology. New information technology changes the methodology of scientific research proper and hence, the understanding of scientific activity" (Ursal, 1989, p. 12). SI emerges as informatics, a scientific and technical discipline that intersects with the social sciences, which focuses on humans and society, providing "in-depth studies of actual trends and patterns in the interaction between society and informatics" (Ursal, 1989, p. 10; Kolin, 2011, p. 460). Informatics becomes social because it is "much closer to such humanities as psychology or sociology, which deal with the complexity of human existence with its unclear essence" (Ursal, 1989, p. 13). It also has a deeply critical impulse, a feature that Day (2007) finds at the core of the version of SI that emerged in the U.S., meaning that researchers must challenge what Ursal (1989, p. 11) sees as the negative consequences of informatisation.

> Practical information activity in our society demonstrates dangerous deformations. These include an almost complete disregard of public opinion, exaggerated optimistic presentation of the current state and silence over errors, widespread deliberate disinformation by giving false (higher) figures, etc. Social (including scientific) information being an important characteristic of society, bears its imprint, since it immediately reflects the state and dynamics of the social system within which it functions.

> To our regret, the above-mentioned task of informatics humanization is recognized with a certain delay, namely, at those stages of informatisation when many negative consequences of this process have clearly manifested themselves. First of all, we mean here an extremely dangerous combination of militaristic and other authoritarian trends with informatisation, as well as economic losses resulting from unauthorized access to computer memories (information thefts, virus-programs, the hecker [sic] movement, etc.).

During the 1990s, Russian scholars advanced their SI agenda nationally and internationally as SI became a course of study in Russian educational institutions and several Departments of SI were established at Moscow State University and the Russian Academy of Sciences, among others (Kolin, 2011, p. 463). Internationally, SI scholars were responsible for content from their report "Social Informatics" becoming part of a proposed course on "Fundamentals of Social Informatics" at the 2nd UNESCO International Congress "Education and Informatics" held in 1994 (UNESCO, n.d.).

Russian SI has been strongly influenced by Ursal's work, as can be seen in its teleological and utopian nature and its goal of identifying and critically analyzing opportunities for human and societal development. His influence is also seen in the desire of SI researchers to foreground the challenges of living in an information society characterized by the increasing pervasiveness of computerization and information and communication technologies (Kolin, 1994, p. 18). However, Ursal's work has not received much attention outside of Russia, despite the fact that his 1989 paper was published in English in a volume of the *International Forum on Information and Documentation*.

A fourth version of SI emerged in the mid 1990s in Japan out of the work of researchers involved in the Japan Association for Social Informatics (JASI) and the Japan Society for Socio-Information Studies (JSIS). Their approach, called "socio-informatics," sought to conceptualize and analyze "information interdisciplinarily and synthetically" (Endo and Abe, 2008, p. 3). These two organizations have taken important steps toward institutionalizing SI in Japan. They have held combined conferences since 2004 and, since 2008, have published the *Journal of Socio-Informatics* (Kurosu, 2010, p. 70), an English-language publication, making their work available to the international SI community for the first time. Yet, the Japanese SI version began much later compared with the previous three versions described here. Its evolution parallels in time the period of transformation in the U.S. version of SI, and may be a possible alternative future for SI. According to the President of the JASI (Kurosu, 2010, p. 73):

> Socio-informatics is, in its essence, a discipline of interdisciplinary and field-crossing nature, which is related to cultural sciences, social sciences and to the field of engineering and that of medicine. Based on this, we are aiming at the construction of a new academism, which deals with the Japanese society and the world in the future by integrating theory and practice.

Japanese SI, like the Russian version, is teleological and utopian. Concerned with the fundamental nature of information, the effects of ICT on social life, and structures and the design of a "good" information society, scholars and researchers in socio-informatics have sought (Endo and Abe, 2008, pp. 3–4):

1. to solve various aspects of production, circulation, accumulation, and use or consumption of information in society;

2. to reconstruct a theoretical framework about a social system from the viewpoint of "Information"; and

3. to search for a relationship between the new information/communication network and social system.

Socio-informatics in Japan has proceeded along three different paths. The earliest and initially most influential type emerged from academic journalism, emphasizing the development of mass communication theory and the analysis of various forms of mass communication media including the Internet and mobile phones (Yoshida, 2008, p. 35). The second path, for which Yoshida (2008, p. 37) takes credit,

> … focuses on the biological revolution that started as an elucidation of DNA information by Watson-Crick, spreading to all areas of life science and bioscience, and which began to develop in biotechnology or bioengineering based upon this spread.

According to Kurosu, (2010, p. 72), this type of socio-informatics seeks to "clarify 'modern characteristics of self organization,' dealing with the information society into which information and information processing permeate" based on "general theories concerning self organization of informatics of social systems." The third type, "fundamental informatics," is proposed by Nishigaki and Takenouchi (2009, p. 81) and focuses on the philosophical foundations of information; its goal is to seek "radical insights into various informational phenomena in biological, mechanical and social fields, rather … basic knowledge of information and communication engineering." Despite their differences, all converge on three shared assumptions: that the social construction and constitution of modern society is based on and is accomplished through interaction with information, that it is important to adopt an information-centered lens to study social phenomena, and that information must always be studied in context because it is generated through the actions of humans and the society in which they live. Interestingly, all of these assumptions reappear in the version of SI that emerged in the U.S. in the mid 1990s and may have been influenced by them.

During the 1990s, six universities in Japan established programs in this new discipline: the Faculty of Social Information at Sappro Gakuin University (1990), the School of Social Information Studies at Otsuma Women's University (1992), the Faculty of Social and Information Studies at Gunma University (1994), the Faculty of Social Information Science at Hiroshima Bunka Gakuin University (1996), the Faculty of Social Information at Jumonji Women's University (1998), and the Department of Social Informatics in the Graduate School of Informatics at Kyoto University (1998). Since then, a School of Social Informatics has been established at Aoyama Gakuin University.

From the ecological perspective, Japanese SI has had a successful, but local, trajectory. A core body of knowledge has been developed and articulated through the collective actions of members of the community and there has been considerable institutionalization with the development of academic programs at multiple locations, professional organizations, and specialized publications. However because of language barriers, the research has not been widely disseminated outside of Japan, which has affected the global impact of this version of SI. In this sense, there are barriers to exchange with the other traditions and Japanese SI thus illustrates isolation, or a low-gene flow situation, due to limitations to exchange and interact within the supra-SI community.

The fifth version of SI emerged in the United Kingdom and, because of local circumstances, has had a different trajectory than those discussed above. Since the 1950s, three decades before the first mention of SI, there has been a prolific and well-established tradition of socio-technical research that has focused on people, technology, and work, primarily from an organizational perspective. Davenport (2008, p. 519) explains that socio-technical research in the U. K. and SI research in the U. S. "share a common interest in the production of technology, and work with complementary concepts and methods, formal links between the two have not been strong for much of the historical period under review." There has, however, been an active community of scholars and researchers in the U.K. focused on SI since the mid 1990s. The University of Edinburgh, Scotland, established a School of Informatics in 1998, drawing on expertise from five units: the Department of Artificial Intelligence, the Centre for Cognitive Science, the Department of Computer Science, the Artificial Intelligence Applications Institute, and the Human Communication Research Centre (School of Informatics, 2014). It has become one of the largest such schools in Europe with over 500 research staff and more than 700 students. Reflecting the diversity of its parts, the mission of the School is the (School of Informatics, 2014):

> … study of the structure, the behaviour, and the interactions of natural and engineered computational systems.
>
> The central focus of Informatics is the transformation of information—whether by computation or communication, whether by organisms or artefacts. Understanding informational phenomena—such as computation, cognition, and communication—enables technological advances.
>
> Informatics has many aspects, and encompasses a number of existing academic disciplines—Artificial Intelligence, Cognitive Science, and Computer Science. Each takes part of Informatics as its natural domain.

Within the school, there is a Social Informatics Cluster, which (Social Informatics Cluster, 2014)

> … works at the intersection of technologies, work practices and organisations, by studying information technologies in their organisational contexts. A multi-disciplinary group that draws on insights from HCI, CSCW, participatory design, organisational sociology and ethnomethodological studies of work, the cluster's activities aim to go beyond traditional ways of developing IT systems, by engaging with IT professionals and breaking down the barriers between IT systems design and use.

There is also a Center for Social Informatics at Edinburgh Napier University, Scotland, affiliated with the Institute for Informatics and Digital Innovation. The Center's mission is "to develop a distinctive body of work that reflects a shared interest in socio-technical interaction at different levels of organisation, and at different stages in the system life cycle" (Center for Social Informatics, 2014). In contrast to the more computationally oriented informatics at the University of Edinburgh, the Center has adopted a working definition of SI and a research focus on organizations, both of which are closely allied with the American version, which will be discussed next.

The sixth and arguably most influential version of SI emerged in the mid 1990s in the U.S. and has had a different trajectory, transcending national boundaries and achieving international reach. Although research about computerization and society had been done for nearly two decades, at that point, by a group of scholars at the University of California at Irvine, including

Kling, the decision to label an approach to studying the social aspects of computing as SI was not made until 1996 by a group of scholars gathered at an NSF-funded Digital Libraries workshop in San Diego (Kling et al., 2005). This happened at a propitious moment because, according to Sawyer and Tapia (2007, p. 264),

> … members of the faculty at the University of California at Irvine (UCI) came together out of common interests in the social aspects of computing. In evolving and expanding discussions, they involved their professional social networks in examining approaches, principles, and venues for showcasing social analyses of computing. This network of social relations centered on the UCI group played a central role in the spread of social informatics—both in the United States and internationally.

As is well known, Kling was a key figure in the rise of SI in the U.S. However, SI did not emerge sui generis from Kling and the UCI group. Sawyer and Tapia (2007, p. 264) explain that the UCI group and information systems researchers in the U.K. and Scandinavia "were known to each other and involved in collaborative projects, conferences, and scholarly debate." In contrast to the isolation of Slovenian, Russian, and Japanese SI, U.S., U.K., and Scandinavian SI researchers interacted and exchanged ideas and scholarship, thereby illustrating an analogue to the horizontal gene transfer exhibited in biological evolution. As is clear from the history provided here, there has been considerable activity among scholars and researchers in many parts of the world who worked in departments and schools of SI established many years prior to the American version. It seems likely that their work, particularly their publications available in English or in translation, would have influenced the American version of SI. Further, in 1989, Kling visited the University of Oslo in Norway, met with Bråten and Roggen, and learned about their new discipline, SI, including "its terms, concepts, theories, models, and research projects carried out by Bråten and his collaborators" (Roggen, 2005). One outcome of this interaction was apparent at the 1996 workshop on digital libraries. Kling and colleagues were discussing a problem: although their research shared a common focus on the complex relationships between computerization and society, they (Kling et al., 2005, p. 30)

> … agreed that the scattering of related research in a wide array of journals and the use of different nomenclatures was impeding both the research and the abilities of "research consumers" to find important work. They decided that a common name for the field would be helpful. After significant deliberation, they selected "social informatics."

The following year, under Kling's direction, many of the same people gathered, at another National Science Foundation funded workshop held at Indiana University in Bloomington, the goal of which was to set a research agenda for SI. One outcome of their work was the definition of SI that has become a widely cited, taken-for-granted, and fundamental assumption of the discipline's core body of knowledge (Kling; 1999, 2003b; Kling et al., 2001; Rosenbaum, 2009). Kling et al. (2005, p. 30) succinctly stated:

> Social informatics refers to the interdisciplinary study of the design, uses and consequences of ICTs that takes into account their interaction with institutional and cultural contexts.

According to Sawyer and Tapia (2007, p. 264), Kling reflected "that the conceptualization of 'social informatics' arose in part as a means to help convey the broad sweep of activities regarding social analyses of computing and to help convey central concepts in this work to computer scientists."

The 1996 and 1997 workshops marked the beginning of a decade and a half of Kling's leadership and much research and professional activity by Kling and colleagues in American SI. Upon joining the School of Library and Information Science (now the Department of Information and Library Science in the School of Informatics and Computing) at Indiana University in 1996, Kling established the first Center for Social Informatics in the U.S.; now renamed the Rob Kling Center for Social Informatics, it continues to be a meeting place for scholars and students interested in SI research. In 1996, Kling and colleagues created a Social Informatics minitrack at the Association for Information Systems annual conference that is still active as the Social Theory in Information Systems Research minitrack. A Special Interest Group for Social Informatics in the Association for Information Science and Technology held its eleventh annual research symposium at the society's annual meeting in 2015. Institutionalizing SI at this scope led to a wide stream of publications, and an active community of scholars. The evolution of the North American version is the focus of the following chapters, in which we describe the core principles, concepts, approaches and methods, findings, and topics of SI.

In this early stage, SI has had a path characterized by fits and starts as research programs, curricula, and academic units developed in different countries between early 1980s and the late 1990s.[4] SI emerged at six different locations, beginning in Norway, then in Yugoslavia (now Slovenia), Russia, Japan, the U.K., and the U.S. While sharing a common interest in the relationship between technology and society, the versions of SI have been somewhat different in each location, reflecting the socio-technical, cultural, political, and other factors that influenced the scholars involved. In all six cases, researchers with shared interests in the study of technology and society engaged in collective action over a number of years to create and establish SI programs, curricula, research centers, and, in some cases, journals and professional organizations in their countries. In short, of the six versions, the North American version has had a competitive advantage because, as is described below, it emerged at the right time and in the right place. American SI researchers worked in academic institutions that were receptive to their work, had access to funding organizations that were willing to sponsor their early attempts at community building, and they were quick to exploit the potential of networked ICT and digital communications as means of disseminating academic research in En-

---

[4]   A more detailed account of the competing sources of SI can be found in Rosenbaum (2014).

glish, the lingua franca of the Internet at that time. It is for these reasons that our text follows with evolutionary stages that are North American centric. Subsequent chapters will describe these stages and will illustrate changes with respect to: principles, approaches, concepts, topics, and findings. It must be pointed out, however, that SI research and teaching continues in all of these locations; while none of the five versions of SI have supplanted the North American version, all remain viable and vital local options for people interested in studying people, ICT, and context.

CHAPTER 3

The Evolution of Social Informatics

As we argued earlier, the most influential version of SI emerged in the U.S. Out of the six early versions, this version of SI has had a different trajectory, and has transcended national boundaries and achieved global reach. It is this version of SI that is the focus of this and the following chapters.

We describe next the evolution of SI in the U.S., from the mid 80s to its current state. In Chapter 3, we describe the evolution of SI through four periods (Sanfilippo and Fichman, 2014). Then, in Chapters 4-8, we focus attention on the evolution of major SI principles (Chapter 4), approaches and methods (Chapter 5), concepts (Chapter 6), topics (Chapter 7), and findings (Chapter 8). In each chapter we demonstrate the evolution through the four developmental stages.

3.1 PERIOD OF FOUNDATIONAL WORK (1980s)

Focusing specifically on the emergence of SI in the U.S., the foundational works can be traced to early critically oriented studies by Kling and colleagues going back in time to the mid 80s. A series of studies by Kling and Iacono (1984a; 1984b; 1988; 1989) sought to empirically test and challenge deterministic discourses surrounding computerization in work and educational settings. Kling and Iacono were particularly interested in the introduction of ICTs into organizations and the impacts these ICTs had on structure, communication, and power in these contexts (1984b; 1988). For example, in their 1984 study of the introduction of a computerized information system into a medium-sized manufacturing firm, Kling and Iacono emphasized how the technology led to structural changes in the hierarchy. Levels of management were condensed, thereby increasing the span of control of remaining managers and increasing their power. This finding was reinforced in their 1988 study of PRINTCO manufacturing. They further asserted that these changes were importantly enabled due to the increased communication and information gathering potential of managers (Iacono and Kling, 1988).

This body of work revealed specific key findings and concepts, which later became central to SI research. Specifically, it emphasized the impact of institutions, organizational politics, and power dynamics on computerization, as well as the multiple and paradoxical impacts of ICTs on people and organizations. Research from this early period was not clearly labeled as a coherent body of SI work, nor did it begin to argue for SI as an approach, but we suggest that it is the origin of the North American version of SI research.

As part of the process of differentiation from other approaches at this stage, SI researchers focused on gap and niche identification, and on the articulation of key principles and concepts that would become the building blocks of SI. The SI principles that were based on these early studies allowed scholars to legitimately account for and engage with different and more diverse concepts than economists, computer scientists, or sociologists would typically address. The economics of technology would likely only consider costs, benefits, and interests and computer scientists would likely only consider the technological features and design; in contrast, SI provided an opportunity for researchers to consider problems from a more holistic and integrated perspective. Evaluation of ICTs from this perspective included emphasis on political, social, and historical dimensions, in addition to technological facets and economic costs. For example, in evaluating the introduction of new information systems, Iacono and Kling (1988) were concerned with patterns of control, decision-making power, social inequalities, organizational culture, and path dependence, including commitments and encumbrances in organizations. Furthermore, SI researchers began to consider computerization at a different scale than would, for example, researchers in the sociology of technology. Whereas sociologists and many social scientists would likely consider social statistics and seek to provide generalizations about computerization success and failure, SI researchers were able to explain what happened at local levels in specific contexts.

Early work in SI provided an opportunity to explain why technological outcomes differ between case studies. However, SI was limited by its relatively nascent stage of scholarship; increased participation and the attention of other scholars were necessary to form a cohesive and legitimate approach to social studies of computing, as an alternative to unverified generalizations and narrow theoretical considerations. It was time to pay attention to the development of coherence in SI research, through internal integration.

3.2   PERIOD OF EXPANSION (1990s)

Throughout the 1990s, SI developed as a perspective from which a variety of interdisciplinary initiatives expanded, forming, by the end of the decade, a relatively cohesive set of principles, clearly labeled as SI. Specifically, during this period social informatics became an area of scholarship explicitly defined by (1) opposition to deterministic perspectives, and (2) a conceptualization of human interactions with ICTs as fundamentally socio-technical.

During this period, SI continued to build its own niche, focusing attention on the internal integration of findings, concepts, terminology, and approaches, as well as the repetition and re-articulation of the early SI principles and concepts; new approaches were also being explored. More scholars became engaged in conducting and disseminating their SI scholarly work. During this period SI began a process of institutionalization with two workshops and a conference mini-track, as well as the establishment of a research center for SI at Indiana University. SI began to fill its niche in the academic ecosystem and attracted enough momentum to overcome future challenges. Researchers began to employ SI to evaluate social aspects of technologies in diverse domains, ranging from a focus on computerization in education and work similar to earlier research (Iacono, 1996; Kling, 1994; 1998; 1999; Kling and Star, 1997), to scholarly communication (Kling, 1997) and the information society (Iacono, 1996; Kling, 1998).

In addition to new topics, new approaches, specific to SI, were proposed. Informational context as a theoretical construct was described and evaluated (Lamb, 1996) and distinct critical and analytical orientations of SI emerged (Kling, 1994; 1998). Core concepts and findings were supported and supplemented as SI research expanded to include additional scholars and collaborators (i.e., Contractor and Seibold, 1993; Kling and Lamb, 1996; 1999). In the 1990s, scholars capitalized on the opportunities established by earlier work and found that analysis employing interdisciplinary theories and methods enabled more productive discussions of topics with which they had long been concerned. SI was becoming more coherent as an approach, under a common label and with a set of ideas and terms to explain common problems. Still it was not yet unified and far from being recognized as a serious approach to the social analysis of computing.

What was established during this period was sustained interest by scholars, providing new opportunities for future collaboration and the consideration of increasingly interdisciplinary and complex research settings. Findings and arguments amassed through the 1990s had not yet been evaluated critically, despite their focus on challenging opposing deterministic arguments and popular discourse. A challenge as SI further developed was internal integration through evaluation and debate around the claims, findings, and theorization resulting from interdisciplinary research on ICT in society.

3.3   COHERENCE

The early 2000s represent the most cohesive point in SI scholarship, yet there was also a foreshadowing of diversification and disagreements as early findings began to be questioned (Agre, 2002). SI was growing more robust, but was also significantly unified in a way that had not happened before 2000. During this period, scholars produced articles, chapters, and entire books devoted to explaining SI. Kling defined SI through a series of revised articles describing it as the "interdisciplinary study of the design, uses, and consequences of ICT that takes into account their interaction with institutional and cultural contexts" (2000a, p. 218). Some version of his definition has appeared in a variety of scholarly publications (e.g., Kling, 2000b; Kling and Hara, 2004; Kling et al., 2005). Kling et al., (2005) argue that SI is an interdisciplinary space for inquiry into similar problems, rather than a new discipline with shared methods and theories; in an effort to expand and clarify this account of SI, they include the SI triangle of technology, institutions, and culture.

Other approaches to explaining SI were developed during this time. For example, Davenport (2005) described SI as contextual "practice-based research" to frame work in organizations in terms of stakeholders, unintended consequences, costs and benefits, interactions, externalities, and environmental variables, barriers, and boundaries. Likewise, Sawyer and Eschenfelder's (2000, p. 428) understanding of SI work was that it "spans issues of design, implementation, and use of ICTs in a wide range of social and organizational settings" and "includes analyses of the impacts of the social and organizational settings on the design, implementation, and uses of ICT; including the intended and unintended social and organizational consequences of ICT-enabled change and change efforts." They claimed "SI research focuses on exploring, explaining, and theorizing about the socio-technical contexts of ICTs." Sawyer and Rosenbaum focused on how SI grounded research in a specific set of principles, and state "SI researchers focus on the social consequences of the design, implementation, and use of ICT over a wide range of social and organizational settings" (2000, p. 89).

It was during this period that Rob Kling's influence was most explicit on the U.S. version of SI. Kling defined SI more concretely then (Kling, 2000a; 2000b) and collaborated prodigiously (i.e., Kling and Callahan, 2003; Kling and Courtright, 2003; Kling and Iacono, 2001; Kling et al., 2003, 2005). His unexpected passing in 2003 brought an outpouring of reflective pieces on his impact on other scholars' work, as well as on the significance of SI (Iacono et al., 2003; Lamb, 2003; Lamb and Sawyer, 2005; Mansell, 2005; Wood-Harper and Wood, 2005). These pieces along with his last published works, coauthored with many of his colleagues, were instrumental in articulation of the core of SI scholarship and added to its coherence.

During this period SI scholarship converged around and contributed to a coherent body of knowledge. Early principles and approaches were refined, and findings and topics provided additional support for SI principles. Specifically, the foundations of SI research and the increased cohesiveness of the community were reinforced by (1) challenges to deterministic narratives, given the increasing prevalence of ICTs in everyday life at the beginning of the 21st century; and (2) development of more robust socio-technical conceptualizations of computerization initiatives. This increased cohesiveness occurred because revisions to and new support from the research of this period supported earlier common dialogue. The coherence of this period was exemplified by Kling et al.'s (2005) book, entitled *Understanding and Communicating Social Informatics*, which synthesized and made explicit the assumptions and findings associated with SI in a single volume. Within this coherent body of research, SI scholars began using more nuanced terminology to allude to sub-areas of SI that had been identified and developed. This period was characterized by internal integration of ideas, a consistent, yet growing group of scholars and the beginning of a coherent pattern of publication venues, a set of relevant conferences, and an institutionalized center.

Kling's position and influence as a central, unifying figure was perhaps the most defining feature of this period. He set a mission and agenda for SI as an area of scholarship, collaborated with many of the other primary scholars, and unified SI through a clear definition and opportunities for dialogue through the Center for Social Informatics at Indiana University, Bloomington, that he founded in 1996. After his untimely death, his legacy inspired publications for years in which authors acknowledged their debts to Kling's principles and seminal works. His death posed an enormous challenge for SI; how to continue and thrive without his critical commentary and contributions. Yet in some ways, there were new opportunities in his wake to challenge and further refine the core principles of SI, as well as to increase scholarship and collaboration in honor of his legacy through the SI institutions and venues he helped to establish.

3.4   PERIOD OF TRANSFORMATION (2006–present)

This period of transformation began as researchers started attaching labels to their work other than SI. Furthermore, very different theoretical approaches were introduced, as scholarship began to address the same problems through different theoretical lenses and from different conceptual perspectives. SI still provided a convenient umbrella term that was being used as an institutional affiliation and disciplinary identity as well as an approach to the study of ICT and the context in which they are designed, implemented, and used. At this time, SI became an established discipline not characterized by much debate over the core ideas, concepts, principles, approaches, and methods as these are now generally assumed. During this period, certain motivations were dropped, including the overt idea of rejecting determinism, either because SI was no longer being seen as tethered to its roots or because the discourse had changed over time; yet many persisted, providing a unifying link to past research. Scholars using SI as an umbrella term brought a wider variety of principles and approaches, and expanded SI topics and findings, crossing over the boundaries of early SI scholarship. Others added new terms and topics, such as group informatics (Goggins et al., 2011), and virtual teams (Shachaf, 2008; 2010; Shachaf and Hara, 2007), along with an increased interest in the social web and online communities of practice (Rosenbaum and Shachaf, 2010; Hara et al., 2010, 2009; Shachaf, 2010). SI scholarship now extended beyond individual case studies to include more comparative works, and at the same time it became further institutionalized, attracting and rewarding new scholars through fellowships to promote SI research and awards for excellence in SI scholarship.

A decade after Kling's passing, a dedicated group of SI scholars continues to engage directly and indirectly with SI's core body of knowledge. For example, Fichman and Rosenbaum's (2014) edited book brings together a group of scholars who reflect on the past, present, and future of SI. In this edited volume, Meyer (2014) and Sawyer and Hartswood (2014) suggest that SI should focus on the hyphen in socio-technical, affording equal importance to the "socio" and the "technical" and thereby differentiating itself from other socio-technical approaches that typically privilege one over the other. Lessard (2014; p. 137), in the same volume, argues that the socio-technical problem should be reframed and that theories of SI should be developed from the grounds of critical realism, an approach that assumes that "patterns of events that we observe in the world are ontologically distinct from the structures, powers, and generative mechanisms that cause them."

Cox (2014) sees another possibility for SI, in a chapter exploring the relevance of the "practice turn" that has occurred in social science theorizing for SI; he seeks to ground SI in "materiality and embodiment; process, routine, and change; social construction and identity; and knowing." In a different book, Sanfilippo and Fichman (2014) argue for moving SI in yet another direction, describing the relationships between ICT and the social/multicultural constructs, articulating various patterns of socio-technical relationships, paying particular attention to SI.

Recent SI scholarship has begun to redefine and reinvent the approach to studying computerization and society. New motivations and new labels differentiate works within the area, just as outmoded and contradicted constructs and concepts have been left behind. For example, Fleischmann (2014; p. 81) makes a persuasive case for the increasingly important role of human values in ICT design and concluding, "SI can make a clearer and stronger case for its usefulness and importance by ensuring that the insights gained through SI are applied back to design, to actively work to make the world a better place." Eschenfelder (2014; p. 101) looks at the ways in which people "arrange and carry out the transfer of intellectual and cultural works" and argues that "use regimes," the "temporary stabilization of networks of associations related to" these activities, provide a unique theoretical framework for SI researchers that turns attention to digital information and cultural artifacts. Taken together, this type of refinement in many ways strengthens the value of this work as rigorous, but in other ways presents a challenge to researchers who consider the same problems in subtly different ways by dividing them into socio-technical studies and SI research.

The tensions felt as the SI domain splinters and is often differentiated from socio-technical studies (Sawyer and Hartswood, 2014) are in some ways mitigated during this period by mutual shaping with social studies of science and community informatics. As these domains borrow from SI and one another, citing key ideas from other traditions, they shape one another. Furthermore, various socio-technical and information systems researchers have drawn in depth on seminal SI works by Kling, Lamb, and Star during this period (e.g., Racherla and Madviwalla, 2013; Stillman and Linger, 2009).

The future of SI brings important opportunities to build on this work, as it provides new models for application in longitudinal, comparative, and larger-scale capacities. SI seems to increasingly be tied to technology, globalization, and larger social and cultural issues surrounding ICT, increasing its cultural relevance and impact and necessitating continued attention.

CHAPTER 4

Principles

Principles refer to the motivations and labels that scholars have used during each stage to describe their scholarly work. Some labels and motives have had a long-lasting impact on SI research throughout these stages while others did not last beyond one particular stage. Notable developments in the principles of SI are presented in Figure 4.1.

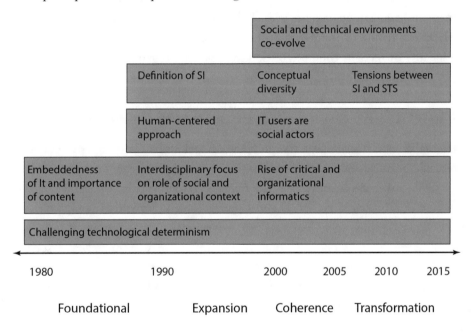

Figure 4.1: Development of principles of SI.

4.1 PRINCIPLES FROM THE FOUNDATIONAL PERIOD (1980S)

In their early works, Kling and Iacono (1984b) challenged deterministic narratives surrounding information system implementation; the reality of a manufacturing firm did not support either socially or technologically deterministic discourses. Instead, empirical evidence supported economically rational arguments explained through metaphors of organizational politics (Kling and Iacono, 1984b). This critical analysis provided more accurate explanations of computerization outcomes than did simplistic deterministic discourses, whether social or technological.

Continued collaboration between Kling and Iacono led to a clear socio-technical principle (1989) that explained the complex interrelationship between social and technical variables (1988), based on their studies of ICTs in organizations. Social theorization about information systems was grounded in case study analysis and described the socio-technical nature of computer-based information systems as being embedded in social and organizational contexts. These systems were found to be highly integrated based on social and technical choices made in the organizations in which the systems were embedded which, in turn, led to the development, implementation, and adoption of the information systems. The socio-technical nature of computerization served as the guiding principle for the developing interdisciplinary nature of SI research.

The period of foundational work has provided SI with two very important principles; SI work (1) challenges deterministic approaches to ICT design, implementation, and use; and (2) embraces the socio-technical nature of computerization in work and education. Through case studies that sought to identify nuances of computerization in social and organizational contexts, SI has been informed by interdisciplinary principles, both in the early stages of development and in the present.

4.2   PRINCIPLES FROM THE PERIOD OF EXPANSION (1990s)

From the onset, researchers studying computerization and society have disagreed about what the discipline should be called and what overarching intellectual principles should guide their inquiries. While the 1990s saw a rise in the use of the terms social informatics (Kling, 1997; 1998; 1999; Kling and Star, 1997; Kling et al., 1998) and organizational informatics (Kling and Lamb, 1999; Kling and Star, 1997; Kling and Tilquist, 1998), other work simply continued to be opposed to technological determinism (Contractor and Seibold, 1993) or was guided by a socio-technical perspective (Kling, 1997; Kling and Lamb, 1996; 1999; Kling et al., 1998). A diversity of principles abounded, ranging from social aspects of ICT (Iacono, 1996; Kling, 1994; 1996; 1998; 1999) to human-centered approaches (Kling and Star, 1997).

SI was defined during the 1990s through the delineation of clear principles (Kling, 1998; Kling et al., 1998). Kling and colleagues sought to encourage interdisciplinary scholars to focus on interactions between ICT and their contexts because ICTs were increasingly tied to social practice, yet were still primarily viewed as tools without embedded social properties (Kling et al., 1998).

Kling and colleagues worked to understand socio-technical interactions (Kling, 1997; Kling and Lamb, 1996; 1999; Kling et al., 1998) and social aspects of ICT (Iacono, 1996; Kling, 1994; 1996; 1998; 1999), in part to better explain new realities surrounding rapid technological change and in part to define SI (Kling et al., 1998). Kling and Lamb (1996; 1999) were interested in how technological services enriched communities. Kling (1997) also articulated a socio-technically grounded strategy for scholarly communities to better benefit from the integration of the Internet and ICT into their work practices.

The embedded social aspects of ICT and the social impacts on ICT design, development, implementation, adoption, and use were of particular interest to SI scholars because at the time common understandings among scholars emphasized technical function and isolated technologies from their creators, controllers, and users (Iacono, 1996; Kling, 1994; 1996; 1998; 1999). Kling (1994; 1996) stressed the need to explore the social possibilities of computerization, rather than functional computing efficiency and productivity alone.

Technological determinism in planning and discourse frustrated an increasing number of scholars (e.g., Contractor and Seibold, 1993). However, their motivation to challenge widely held assumptions about ICTs was not limited to determinism; Kling and Star (1997) collaborated in proposing human-centered approaches to design, as they were opposed to design for function rather than use.

Guiding principles varied in name and specificity, yet additional scholars were drawn to the same issues that Kling and Iacono had earlier considered. Not only were the conversation and focus developing, but, by the end of the 1990s, it was clear that the works were related and beginning to converge around the discipline of SI.

This period of expansion provided SI with a re-articulation and refining of some early principles, such as, SI work: (1) challenges deterministic approaches; and (2) embraces the socio-technical nature of computerization in work, education, society, and scholarly communities. Furthermore, early patterns were formalized as principles: (3) SI work pays attention to the importance of social and organizational contexts; and (4) the interaction between ICT and the context matters. At the same time additional principles were added, such as: (5) SI focuses on the social aspects of technology; (6) SI work brings a human-centered approach to ICT design, development, implementation, and use; and (7) ICTs are not value neutral.

4.3   PRINCIPLES FROM THE PERIOD OF COHERENCE (2000–2005)

The labels employed for SI research continued to vary. In particular, two approaches continued to be employed to describe the principles from which SI research was conducted: opposition to determinism (Agre, 2002; Meyer and Kling, 2002; Lamb and Sawyer, 2005) and the socio-technical construct (e.g., Kling, 2000a; 2000b; Sawyer and Rosenbaum, 2000). These fundamental approaches continued to be useful as determinism and the separate treatment of social and technical variables persisted in specific areas of society, such as politics; for example, Agre sought to address the failings of political arguments based on limited understanding of the Internet by demonstrating the applicability of the technology in binding polities without fundamentally altering social structure (2002). Meyer and Kling (2002) sought to correlate technological determinism with what they called "standard models," providing socio-technical constructs as socially rich, internally coherent, alternatives to both.

Kling and his colleagues emphasized the differentiation between standard and socio-technical models (Kling, 2000b; Kling and Callahan, 2003; Kling et al., 2003). Socio-technical models were the basis for a new practically oriented principle of SI, through which strategies for socio-technical change could be successfully identified and executed, such as in the e-journal domain (Kling and Callahan, 2003). This practically oriented conceptualization surrounding interactions between technology and people also allowed for explanations as to why parallel developments led to divergent outcomes, as in scholarly communication patterns mediated by ICT (Kling and McKim, 2000).

In this sense, the meaning of the socio-technical construct was evolving to further encompass related, previously peripheral principles of SI scholarship. The identification of social and technical facets of context and interaction was commonly used by SI scholars to illustrate socio-technical principles in research areas including rural telecommunication expansion in developing nations (Courtright, 2004), the boundaries of communities of practice (Hara and Kling, 2002; Kling and Courtright, 2003), mobile computing work in policing (Sawyer and Tapia, 2005), and libraries in the Internet age (Kling, 2001). Complex, nested, and socially constructed contexts of cultural, organizational, and relational facets also framed and influenced technology in the socio-technical principle (Kling, 2000a; 2000b); for example, Lamb and Davidson argued that ICT are socially embedded (2005). Kling provided and expanded upon a specific socio-technical model in which core SI findings underlie the principle (Kling, 2000b), and later argued that it must be included in education models for information professionals (Kling, 2003b; Kling et al., 2005).

SI, as a discipline, has constantly been redefined but stabilized to an extent during this period; Lamb and Sawyer defined SI in terms of its history of opposition to simplistic, deterministic arguments, as well as its socio-technical orientation (2005). Lamb specifically attributed the growing significance of SI to Kling's socio-technical studies (Lamb, 2003); in their joint work, they emphasized the socio-technical construct as grounded in the SI findings that ICT users are primarily social actors (Lamb and Kling, 2003).

Specific informatics-centered labels were popularized in addition to SI, including: critical informatics (Iacono et al., 2003; Kling, 2003b; Lamb and Sawyer, 2005), and organizational informatics (Kling, 2000a; Kling and Hara, 2004; Sawyer and Eschenfelder, 2002; Sawyer and Rosenbaum, 2000), which dates back to the 1980s but became more prevalent during this period, among others.

During this period, within SI, sub-domains were being carved out. Kling (2003b) described his own approach as critical informatics. Iacono et al. (2003) and Lamb and Sawyer (2005) agreed and applied the term critical informatics to describe Kling's work and legacy and a subset of SI work, employing the critical orientation to empirically test all possibilities, rather than depending upon shared expectations or vocabulary common to SI content alone.

Organizational informatics, "those SI analyses bounded within organizations—where the primary participants are located within identifiable organizations" (Sawyer and Rosenbaum, 2000, p. 90), was also coalescing within SI (Kling, 2000a; Kling and Hara, 2004; Sawyer and Eschenfelder, 2002; Sawyer and Rosenbaum, 2000). Kling and Hara defined organizational informatics as a "subfield of SI that focuses upon 'the design, uses and consequences of IT that takes into account their interaction with organizations" (2004, p. 2).

As another SI sub-domain, educational informatics was defined as "the awareness, development, and synthesis of appropriate pedagogies for these IT-enabled 'learning environments,' and also the consequences of different approaches for... participants" in these environments (Kling and Hara, 2004, p. 1). SI as a guiding perspective in interdisciplinary social computing research was applied often enough during this period to the educational domain to distinguish this sub-domain of SI, in part because of the number of contributing scholars and in part because of the diverse interests of and applications by researchers.

Furthermore, discussions of the social aspects of ICT not only persisted, but also were pervasive (e.g., Davenport, 2000; 2001; Hara and Kling, 2002; Iacono et al., 2003; Kling and McKim, 2000). Sawyer and Eschenfelder (2002) emphasized the importance of developing and extending social theory to explain how ICT are influenced by and used in social contexts. Scholars were fundamentally concerned with context-sensitive approaches (Sawyer and Eschenfelder, 2002) because social relationships and interactions are tightly coupled to technologies (Allen, 2005). With the goal of understanding the success, consequences, challenges, and failures of ICT implementation and use, research based on the principle that ICT cannot be isolated from their environments generated empirical evidence that could explain value conflicts (Allen, 2005), types of support (Davenport, 2000), and situated information flow (Davenport, 2001) in complex organizations.

Social variables were recognized as not being obfuscated by technology, but rather social and technical environments were seen to co-evolve before and after ICT implementation (Kling et al., 2005). Deconstructing practice through SI principles allows the social (Ekbia and Kling, 2005; Hara and Kling, 2002; Kling and McKim, 2000), political (Mansell, 2005), and economic (Ekbia and Kling, 2005; Mansell, 2005) boundaries and limitations of context to be equally examined, rather than be relegated to the status of footnotes in the study of function.

By fostering socially rich dialogue surrounding ICT, analysis became more nuanced, strengthening critical informatics. What began in earlier research as a critical orientation became something more formalized as a critical perspective (Lamb and Sawyer, 2005); in addition, human-centered principles (Kling et al., 2005; Lamb and Kling, 2003; Sawyer, 2005) expanded to include usability concerns from other areas of information science, specifically human-computer interaction and information architecture (Kling et al., 2005; Lamb and Kling, 2003). Framing SI analyses by acknowledging the people who design and use ICT provides better design and policy solutions (Kling et al., 2005).

In sum, this period of coherence saw the increasing adoption and use of additional modifiers besides "social" informatics, including: critical informatics, organizational informatics, and educational informatics. During the early years of 21st century SI became more coherent as scholars continued with the re-articulation and refining of some early principles, such as the notions that SI work: (1) challenges deterministic approaches; (2) embraces the socio-technical nature of computerization in a variety of settings; (3) pays attention to the importance of context as the interaction between ICT and context matters; (4) focuses on the social aspects of technology; and (5) brings a human-centered approach to ICT design, development, implementation, and use. The guiding principles of SI were most sound and well structured during this period. The development of specific sub-domains indicated the impact and level of participation in this area of scholarship, perhaps foreshadowing the establishment of SI as a scholarly discipline. Momentum developed for continued participation and attention to socio-technical problems and changes.

4.4   PRINCIPLES OF THE TRANSFORMATIONAL PERIOD (2005–present)

The principles guiding SI work, nearing the present, include diverse labels: the socio-technical (e.g., Contractor et al., 2011; Davenport, 2008; Goggins et al., 2011; King et al., 2007; Sawyer and Tyworth, 2006; Tapia and Maitland, 2009), as an alternate but complementary approach to traditional SI (Davenport, 2008; Day, 2007; Elliot and Kraemer, 2007; Fichman and Rosenbaum, 2014; Sanfilippo and Fichman, 2014; Oltmann et al., 2006; Sawyer and Tapia, 2007; Sawyer and Tyworth, 2006); social aspects of ICT (Contractor, 2009; Davenport and Horton, 2006; 2007; Day, 2007; Elliot and Kraemer, 2007; Fichman and Hara, 2014; Robbin and Day, 2006; Shachaf and Hara, 2007; Wade, 2014); critical informatics (Day, 2007; King et al., 2007); the critical perspective (King et al., 2007; Robbin and Day, 2006); and usability (Oltmann et al., 2006).

While this work is labeled in at least six different ways, there are two that have been more prominent in recent scholarship: SI and the socio-technical. For many researchers, the domains designated by these labels overlap and are equally relevant for their own academic contributions (Lessard, 2014), yet for others both differ in their relevance and legitimacy as descriptions of their scholarship. This seemingly indicates that what began as one interdisciplinary set of SI principles is transforming and expanding around the earlier principles. There is a simultaneous trend toward borrowing from SI, along with other traditions, in a blending of principles, as in the case of community informatics, which draws on SI and information systems principles and research (Shin and Shin, 2012; Stillman and Linger, 2009). There has been further scholarship into online communities of practice (e.g., Rosenbaum and Shachaf, 2010; Hara et al., 2010, 2009); these studies have expanded early concepts that had been organizationally bounded in prior periods into the social web and open communities (Fichman and Hara, 2014).

While during this period of transformation, scholars have used SI as an umbrella term to indicate identity and institutional affiliation, some have moved away from using SI terminology. It has become evident to many other scholars that there is no longer a need to re-articulate early ideas that challenged deterministic approaches, perhaps because SI has reached a point where the challenge is no longer needed; the discourse has moved beyond the issue of determinisms. These early principles, 15 years later, have become taken for granted.

A decade after Kling's passing, a group of scholars published SI works (Fichman and Rosenbaum, 2014) that not only emphasize early principles but also suggest new ones. On one hand, SI has focused on redefining and reinventing the approach to studying computerization and society and the motivations that have been left behind. For example, the increasingly important role of human values in ICT design ensures that the early insights gained through SI research will be "applied back to design, to actively work to make the world a better place" (Fleischmann, 2014). SI work continues to focus much attention on the social aspects of technology and brings a human-centered approach to issues of ICT design, implementation, and use. This type of refinement in many ways strengthens SI. Likewise, SI researchers continue to attend to the importance of context because the interaction between ICT and context continues to matter; complexity and paradox are routinely integrated into SI works (Shachaf, and Hara, 2007). The guiding principles of SI are still evident and there is continued attention to socio-technical problems and dynamics, but with much less need to revisit and re-evaluate the core body of SI knowledge.

On the other hand, at this point in time, SI scholars are beginning to focus specifically on new directions that will differentiate SI from other socio-technical approaches. For example, Meyer (2014) focuses on the hyphen in socio-technical, affording equal importance to the "socio" and the "technical" while Sawyer and Hartswood (2014) sketch out a path involving working on larger and more complex projects with larger research teams that innovate methodologically, toward a goal of developing a rich and compelling social and technologically grounded vision of the future. At the same time, Sanfilippo and Fichman (2014) describe the relationships between ICT and the socio-cultural constructs, articulating a wide variety of patterns of socio-technical relationships, under the SI framework. Others have argued that the socio-technical problem should be reframed and that theories of SI should be developed from the grounds of critical realism (Lessard, 2014). Yet, another possibility for SI is to ground it in practice-studies that centralize around (1) process, routine, and change; (2) social construction and identity; and (3) knowing (Cox, 2014).

CHAPTER 5

Approaches and Methods

Approaches refer to the theories, frameworks, and models that SI scholars employ in their analyses, while *Methods* include both research designs and techniques. The utilization of multiple and varied theories emphasizes the multi-disciplinary and interdisciplinary nature of SI throughout the four stages. Furthermore, while it is clear that there are no unifying methods within this work, SI has largely depended on small, qualitative studies throughout its development.

5.1 APPROACHES AND METHODS FROM THE FOUNDATIONAL PERIOD

This early research represents the varied, deeply interdisciplinary approaches emblematic of SI that continue to feature in SI research. Kling and Iacono (1984a; 1984b; 1988; 1989) came to their findings through institutional social shaping approaches, political analysis, and the introduction of both a computerization movement framework and socio-technical studies. These diverse approaches represent the indefinite theoretical boundaries of SI; the theoretical approaches used in SI research represent a variety of disciplines, from which SI scholars borrow to study and explain their work. However, a commonality throughout these studies was there dependence on document analysis and interviews within the case studies analyzed in each project (e.g., Kling and Iacono, 1984b; 1989).

An institutional social shaping approach to the study of computing in organizations is manifested through both institutional and organizational theory (Kling and Iacono, 1984a; 1989). Institutional theory underlies social control models, which explain how management and control structures impact computerization by accounting for information flows, actors, controls, and rule systems (Kling and Iacono, 1984a). Organizational theory is the foundation for social organization of computing models; ICTs are situated in social structures and boundaries are shaped by social, rather than technical parameters (Kling and Iacono, 1984a). Closely correlated with the understanding and evaluation of social structures is political analysis; Kling and Iacono (1984b) made use of elements of political theory—including coalition formation, ideologies and preferences, mobilization of support, and legitimacy—to explain how computing infrastructure can be controlled by dominant parties or shared governance.

Computerization movements were developed as a theoretical construct and empirically evaluated by Kling and Iacono (1988) in order to characterize general beliefs and practices, as well as to differentiate between specific attributes of various mobilizations for support of computerization. Modeled on theories of social movements, the construct holds that computerization movements are fragmentary in nature, have shared core beliefs, and treat particular computer-based technologies as inherently different from other, older innovations; they involve value-laden arguments made by computerization movement advocates that allow for deconstruction of mismatches between context and technologies in cases of unmet expectations (Kling and Iacono, 1988). This conceptualization was supported by meta-analysis of the literature relating to five distinct types of computerization movements that had been studied at that point: urban information systems, artificial intelligence, ICTs in education, the automation of work and office routines, and personal computing (Kling and Iacono, 1988).

Socio-technical studies, as derived from work by Kling and Iacono (1989), are based on empirically grounded social theories about computerization that explain unanticipated outcomes, both in terms of change and stasis. Socio-technical studies consider information systems, and technologies, in the context of mutually shaping social and technical factors (Kling and Iacono, 1989).

Theoretical designs developed and employed by Kling and Iacono (1984a; 1984b; 1988; 1989) represent the value of SI approaches to business, political, and social problems in comparison to approaches to these problems posed by more traditional domains of scholarship. SI, from the beginning, was not bound by a single theory. Kling and Iacono were early to draw on theories from other disciplines, in order to theorize about ICT in organizational contexts.

5.2   APPROACHES AND METHODS FROM THE PERIOD OF EXPANSION

To explain these findings, a variety of theoretical constructs were employed including newly proposed approaches for SI, specifically, the critical (Kling, 1994; 1996) and analytical orientations (Kling, 1996), as well as the informational context (Lamb, 1996). The institutional social shaping approach continued to be employed (Lamb, 1996), as in earlier work, yet different constructs were also transferred to SI work, including structuration and systems theory (Contractor and Seibold, 1993; Kling and Star, 1997). During this period, the qualitative case study tradition was also continued, yet SI branched out into additional qualitative methods, including discourse analysis (e.g., Kling, 1994; Kling and Lamb, 1999) and policy analysis (e.g., Kling and Tilquist, 1998).

The introduction of specific orientations in SI, the critical and the analytical, was significant because these orientations structured SI work and legitimated different kinds of approaches and motivations in SI research. The critical orientation developed from the earliest SI impulses to challenge thin arguments about technology and computerization through robust empirically supported counter-arguments (i.e., Kling, 1994; 1996). The analytical orientation sought to understand specific instances of socio-technical interaction, in order to make sense of changes in computerization (Kling, 1996). These distinct orientations had important implications for research designs and epistemology because the critical orientation required richer data and normative and analytically oriented works reflected positivist and interpretive epistemologies.

Further, during this period, Lamb (1996) developed one of the earliest socio-technical theories within SI: that of the informational context. Informational imperatives, common in discourse, emphasized accelerated rationality, empowered democracy, increased digitization, and streamlined bureaucracy, yet did not explain real behaviors or changes, leading Lamb (1996) to conceptually reframe the social potential of ICT as technologically mediating interpersonal interactions for more effective interaction at a distance and providing access to power.

The introduction of structuration into SI work was also significant at this stage, because it supported the understandings of the social shaping of technology (Contractor and Seibold, 1993). Systems theory, in the form of human-centered systems (HCS) theory also contributed to SI insights through the analysis of: the intertwining of the social and the technical; continued, longitudinal, and iterative development through use; complex human and machine interactions; and the inclusion of users and beneficiaries in development, design, evaluation, and use of ICT (Kling and Star, 1997). Specifically, the advantage of this approach was that it allowed for the conceptualization of people, technology, and contexts as integrated systems that persist over time; HCS theory considers systems to be:

1. based on an analysis of the human tasks that the system is aiding

2. monitored for performance in terms of human benefits

3. built to take account of human skills and

4. adaptable easily to changing human needs. (Kling and Star, 1997, p. 22)

The interdisciplinary theories and the new SI theorization of this period of research increasingly bolstered the objectives of SI: to improve design and understand the actual uses and consequences of ICT, rather than to simply explain design prescriptions or outcomes from a particular set of disciplinary theories. This served as an ideal set up for ideas of mutual shaping introduced into SI through the importation of several theoretical perspectives, notably structuration theory.

5.3   APPROACHES FROM THE PERIOD OF COHERENCE

Various theoretical constructs from earlier research continued to shape analyses and a number of different theories were introduced during this period. Between 2000 and 2005, there was clear emphasis on political and economic aspects of socio-technical interactions (Agre, 2000b; Ekbia and Kling, 2005; Mansell, 2005) from a theoretical perspective, while from a methodological perspective, socio-technical interaction network (STIN) analysis was developed. There was also growing interest in the concept of networks in SI theorizing (Lamb and Davidson, 2005), specifically emphasizing actor-network theory (e.g., Hara and Kling, 2002; Sawyer and Tapia, 2005), in analysis (Courtright, 2005), and as basis for conceptualizing socio-technical networks (e.g., Kling, 2000a; Kling et al., 2003; Lamb, 2003).

Institutional theory (Lamb and Davidson, 2005) and institutional social shaping approaches (Agre, 2000a) continued to ground research. The social shaping of technology (SST), arguably a socially deterministic approach, complimented this work and began to form a more concrete theoretical approach which would continue to grow in popularity beyond this period (Kling and McKim, 2000; Sawyer and Tapia, 2005). Socio-technical theory, because of its focus on mutually shaping tendencies, provided a more balanced perspective on social and technical interactions than did social shaping theory (Lamb and Kling, 2003; Sawyer and Tapia, 2005), and formalized the socio-technical considerations of earlier studies (Lamb and Sawyer, 2005).

One major research trend in this period was an emphasis on economic and political issues that complemented SI's traditional emphasis on the design and policy implications of empirically sound arguments (Kling, 2000a; 2000b). Economic theory (Agre, 2000b; Ekbia and Kling, 2005; Mansell, 2005)—specifically as a theory of economies of scale (Agre, 2000b), a theory of the networked society with respect to production relationships (Ekbia and Kling, 2005), and rationality, through theories of political economy (Mansell, 2005)—provided explanations of institutional and individual behaviors and financial interests regarding investment in technology and the benefits of ICT innovation and adoption. By explaining informational, global, and networked attributes of ICT, economic theory could explain complexity and provide predictive modeling for strategic planning surrounding ICT (Ekbia and Kling, 2005). Political analysis complements these approaches by explaining resistance to and enforcement of institutional and organizational norms, including strategic practices (Mansell, 2005).

The second major trend focused on networks, which was in some ways correlated with the economic theory of networked society (Ekbia and Kling, 2005), as well as being based in the understanding that ICT users are social actors (Lamb and Davidson, 2005; Lamb and Kling, 2003). Network theory, emphasizing the importance of relationships and interactions between actors, institutions, and information resources, deconstructed the use of ICT for collaboration and coordination to a conceptual level (Lamb and Davidson, 2005). The importation of actor-network theory, as one manifestation of network approaches, facilitated analysis at a level that focuses on important nodes, socio-technical processes, and specific interactions in a network, as opposed to exhaustively attempting to explain all nodes and interactions (Hara and Kling, 2002; Kling et al., 2003; Lamb and Kling, 2003; Sawyer and Tapia, 2005). Network analysis not only emphasized relationships between nodes, but also provided a modeling mechanism to characterize types of relationships and the central importance of specific nodes within communities, as in Courtright's (2005) study of social health-information seeking of Latino immigrants through face-to-face interaction and technologically mediated interaction. Courtright (2005) employed semi-structured interviews to examine public services and health care information exchanges. From this data, networks were constructed to examine how information flowed within the bounded communities in which participants were embedded.

Socio-technical interaction network (STIN) analysis provides an SI-specific mechanism to explore networks of people and ICTs. Kling et al. (2003) employ STIN modeling to examine on-line professional communications as computer-mediated scholarly communication. They argue that STIN provides a mechanism that more richly illustrates lifecycle and uses of online communities by explicitly illustrating how gatekeeping and integration issues define interactions and flow. STIN explicitly applied network theory to socio-technical contexts by including technologies as nodes, in addition to mechanisms that facilitate interactions or relationships between actors, groups, and resources (Kling, 2000a; Kling et al., 2003; Lamb, 2003; Meyer and Kling, 2002). This contextual application established socio-technical network models in SI research, including the social actor model, to more accurately account for the mutually shaping interactions between social and technical factors (Kling and Callahan, 2003; Lamb and Davidson, 2005; Lamb and Kling, 2003; Meyer and Kling, 2002). Furthermore, STIN provided a distinct research design in addition to serving as the basis for analysis.

Other SI-specific approaches developed during this period include technical action frames (Kling and Iacono, 2001), information environments (Lamb et al., 2003), and the multiview approach (Wood-Harper and Wood, 2005). These theoretical developments recognized the importance of grounding discourse about ICT design, implementation, and use in empirical realities for successful practical outcomes (Kling and Iacono, 2001), the institutional and technical dimensions of workplaces as ICT interaction contexts (Lamb et al., 2003), and the insight that the complexity of socio-technical innovation, implementation, and change can only be explained through multivariate theoretical combinations, not through reductive, simplifying constructs (Wood-Harper and Wood, 2005).

SI has long emphasized social theory and theorizing about ICT and computerization (Sawyer and Eschenfelder, 2002), and this has been manifested in a variety of ways including the use of the amplification model (Agre, 2002), grounded theory (Allen, 2005), activity theory (Davenport, 2005), and regimes of truth (Ekbia and Kling, 2003). Grounded theory approaches to research design have importantly led to the development of key SI theories, such as Allen's (2005) schema for enterprise resource planning (ERP) based on value conflicts. Allen (2005) specifically employed ethnography, interviews, and documental analysis in order to understand conflicts in design in a medium-sized computing input hardware firm and through a participant observer approach, a rich understanding of the context was developed. In tandem with many of these specific theories, analysis of SI research has described critical (Iacono et al., 2003; Kling, 2003b; Lamb and Sawyer, 2005; Sawyer and Rosenbaum, 2000), normative (Lamb and Sawyer, 2005; Sawyer and Rosenbaum, 2000), and analytical orientations (Lamb and Sawyer, 2005; Sawyer and Rosenbaum, 2000). Earlier work had primarily been analytical or critical, but the third orientation—normative—provided more practical and tangible translations of SI research as providing implications for design, policy, and/or use alternatives (Lamb and Sawyer, 2005).

Diverse approaches and methods during this period resulted in part from the increased visibility of SI and its central scholars in other disciplines, drawing in communication and media scholars, who were relatively closely aligned in some respects, as well as scholars of the political economy who generally dealt with specific concepts that were distinct from SI despite some overlap of attention to similar problems. The increasing complexity of the structure of SI, in identifying the normative orientation, was also a significant step toward institutionalization and important in validating and including different types of scholarship in shared discussion.

5.4   APPROACHES AND METHODS FROM THE TRANSFORMATIONAL PERIOD

Recent research has diversified and revised theoretical approaches and methods of analysis from SI perspectives. While there continues to be interest in network theory and analysis (i.e., Contractor, 2009; Goggins et al., 2011) and technical action frames (Davenport and Horton, 2006; 2007; Robbin et al., 2006), older constructs, such as computerization movements, have been revised (Hara and Rosenbaum, 2008), and new theories, such as IS/IT governance theory (Maldonado et al., 2010), have been developed.

Networks, as a theoretical construct, enable social informaticians, or SI scholars, to look at the relationships among individuals, institutions, and ICT in order to identify patterns and understand the contexts of socio-technical interaction (Contractor, 2009; Sawyer and Tyworth, 2006). Network-centered methodologies have also grown in popularity, consistent with their employment in other domains of research. These works can be subdivided in a number of ways: general network analysis, actor network analysis, STIN modeling, and information diffusion networks, as exemplified by those constructed by Courtright (2005). The analysis of networks (Goggins et al., 2011) is guided by a variety of approaches, including the socio-technical network model (Blincoe et al., 2012), social network theory (Contractor, 2009), actor-network theory (Contractor, 2009; Contractor et al., 2011; Davenport, 2008), and STINs (Sawyer and Tyworth, 2006). Blincoe et al. (2012), for example, exemplify the general adaptation of quantitative network analysis and visualization to explore proximity as an antecedent to coordination within organizational contexts. STIN analysis has also been applied, for example, by Meyer (2006) employed to study marine biologists, and by Shachaf and Rosenbaum (2009) to analyze online social reference.

Actor Network Theory, often used in social studies of science and socio-technical studies, has also been popular in SI. Davenport (2008) provides an example in which this theory guides network analysis in tandem with the novel ETHICS methodology for analysis. ETHICS, as the effective technological and human implementation of computer systems, is a socio-technical framework to guide systematic analysis of interactions between people and ICT in the implementation process, which is a common focus within SI scholarship. Network analysis importantly supports this method because it conceptualizes interactions in a way that can be systematically interpreted.

Socio-technical theory is also developing into a multi-theoretical and integrated framework for studies of interactions (Davenport, 2008; Racherla and Mandviwalla, 2013) based on principles of mutual shaping between social contexts, uses, and technologies (Sawyer and Tyworth, 2006; Tapia and Maitland, 2009). The socio-technical systems (STS) construct, in particular, is developing into a popular mechanism for the conceptualization of information systems because it enables and mutually impacts social processes (Tapia and Maitland, 2009; Singh, 2013).

Governance issues, addressed by IS/IT governance theory, have increasingly become a focus of analysis because of their control and power implications surrounding access and changes to ICT (Maldonado et al., 2010). IS/IT governance theory was derived in part from multi-level governance theory, as a subarea of political theory (Maldonado et al., 2010). Political theory and political economics, involving, for example, rational actor theory (Robbin and Day, 2006), are employed in a variety of ways to explain the interests of stakeholders and the distributions of computerization outcomes (Maldonado et al., 2010; Robbin, 2007).

A variety of other social theories have been imported from other fields to support the interdisciplinary inquiries of SI (Robbin, 2007), including articulation work (Sawyer and Tapia, 2006), institutional theory (Sawyer and Tpaia, 2007), organizational theory (Tapia and Maitland, 2009), and structuration (Rosenbaum and Shachaf, 2010), as well as information worlds (Burnett et al., 2014), the practice approach (Cox, 2014), textual criticism (Simpson, 2014), and critical realism (Lessard, 2014). Within the domain of SI, specifically constructed social theories include behavioral complexity theory of media selection (Shachaf and Hara, 2007), as well as social theories of learning in the context of ICT (Goggins et al., 2007).

Research from the beginning of this period has used critical orientations to focus on cases, trends, and SI itself (Day, 2007; King et al., 2007; Oltmann et al., 2006; Robbin and Day, 2006). The theoretical approaches employed to further SI in recent years are reflective of the desire to revise, fortify, and institutionalize SI as a significant and advantageous approach to the analysis of social aspects of computing (Sawyer and Tpaia, 2007). There is also a movement, driven by Orlikowski and Iacono (2008), to redirect attention away from context and use, toward the IT artifact itself, to understand its meaning, potential, functions, and embedded properties, rather than to simply the consequences of IT; IT theory, as a standalone technical theory, is beginning to emerge.

Many of these theoretical approaches have applied relevant theories from other domains and have drawn on rich theoretical developments from many disciplines to define integrated multi-theoretical frameworks to inform SI research. Furthermore, interdisciplinary interactions with SI research has led to changes in methodological norms, as the popularity of network analysis in particular has led to the introduction of quantitative analysis in SI. The value in these developments is that scholars frame their work more in SI terms, while continuing to be comprehensible and relevant to scholars in other domains considering the same issues.

CHAPTER 6

Concepts

Concepts refer to the specific elements of discourse within a given context, revealing a shared SI language surrounding change, complexity, consequences, and social elements of technology. These include specific processes, entities, and themes; some of which become more prominent than others within the SI discourse. A chronology of conceptual development over time, denoting key references in the development, is provided in Table 6.1.

6.1 CONCEPTS FROM THE FOUNDATIONAL PERIOD

With these interdisciplinary theories and frameworks, Kling and Iacono articulated their core findings through the analysis of key SI concepts including: change (1988), complexity (1989), context (1984a), control (1984a; 1984b; 1989), efficiency (1989), institutions (1984a; 1989), management (1984a; 1989), organizational politics (1984b; 1989), power relationships (1984b; 1989), and values (1988).

Social context is important in evaluating technological outcomes because the actors, rules, interactions, and processes surrounding technologies shape ICT, while being shaped by them (Kling and Iacono, 1984a). Organizational contexts are of particular importance because of their scale and organizations' early-mover roles in adopting new technologies (Kling and Iacono, 1984a; 1989). Institutions and organizations are also particularly complex as they seek to achieve efficiency, productivity, and profitability through the introduction of technology and managed change (Kling and Iacono, 1984a; 1988; 1989). Early SI work, particularly the collaborations between Iacono and Kling, treated institutions and organizations as somewhat analogous, with institutions referring to public and bureaucratic organizations; later work differentiated between the constructs, with institutions as the implicit and explicit rules that created social structure, with continued emphasis on both concepts.

Management and control create disparities and unequal distributions of authority, information, and access to technologies (Kling and Iacono, 1984a; 1984b; 1989). From disparities come conflict within organizational and institutional contexts (Kling and Iacono, 1984b); a common resolution of conflict is ICT change or stasis that favors the status quo because those in power seek to maximize their own benefits in advocating for, controlling, and preventing changes (Kling and Iacono, 1984a; 1984b; 1988).

Organizational politics and power relationships elegantly reveal the extent to which ideologies and influence impact ICT outcomes (Kling and Iacono, 1984b; 1989), just as social values create norms, as well as barriers to the compromise of social values, which also impact ICT outcomes (Kling and Iacono, 1988). Values, in addition to shaping commitments to and uses of technologies in contexts that may or may not be amenable to ICT change, are embedded in the ICT themselves (Kling and Iacono, 1988).

From these concepts, the vocabulary of SI developed. Conceptual themes unified the focus of Kling and Iacono's work, as well as that of future studies; SI scholars are still concerned with similar problems, including the same concepts in different and unique configurations.

6.2   CONCEPTS FROM THE PERIOD OF EXPANSION

Growing interests and concerns with all possible variables affecting outcomes of computerization in diversifying domains were reflected in the concepts considered. Understanding the complex reality of change in socio-technical environments continued to be a major concern and was reflected in the specific conceptual language of change (Contractor and Seibold, 1993; Iacono, 1996; Kling, 1994; 1996; Kling and Tilquist, 1998; Kling et al., 1998), complexity (Kling, 1996; 1999; Kling and Star, 1997; Kling and Tilquist, 1998), and context (Kling, 1996; 1998; 1999; Kling and Star, 1997; Kling and Tilquist, 1998; Lamb, 1996).

SI research addressed the role of ICT in social and organizational change (Kling et al., 1998). Change was analyzed in terms of the impact of technological change on social structures in organizations (Contractor and Seibold, 1993), as well as how social change shaped the information age (Iacono, 1996). Kling analyzed computerization movements in order to understand change in both directions, in terms of the social choices that yield technological change and the impact of new computer technologies on social organization (Kling, 1994; 1996). Kling emphasized that expectations of positive change, and change in general, are often unmet (1996). Collaborating with Tilquist, he went on to illustrate why technology-driven organizational change often failed, arguing, for example, that the precepts of business process reengineering emphasized top-down directives to stakeholders, non-contextual solutions, and imposed constraints on the legitimacy of non-technical solutions (Kling and Tilquist, 1998).

Anticipated changes failed to materialize and unanticipated changes occurred precisely because organizations, institutions, and technology were much more complex than simplistic arguments acknowledged (Kling and Tilquist, 1998). Part of the complexity could be explained as mismatches in embedded social variables between the technologies, embodying social facets from their contexts of development, and the social contexts in which they are used (Kling, 1996). Furthermore, complexity developed from multiple levels of implicit and explicit work practices, norms, supports, and constraints (Kling, 1999), as well as variable scopes, large scales, and externalities manifesting change over time (Kling and Star, 1997).

In context, outcomes were different because no combinations of workers, technologies, environments, and points in time are the same (Kling and Star, 1997). The real problem with business process re-engineering during this period was its failure to account for the influence of different contexts (Kling and Tilquist, 1998). In not acknowledging context, imperatives about change through ICT prescribed unrealistic expectations on which public policies were produced, leading to public failures on a large scale (Lamb, 1996). What SI successfully provided was an analytical lens grounded in real complexity, rather than over-simplified non-empirical prescriptions (Kling, 1996; 1998; 1999).

Building on concepts of complexity and changes over time, dynamics were introduced as an important concept (Kling, 1997; Kling and Star, 1997) resulting from multiple sets of norms and practices interacting within a context (Kling, 1997). Externalities, time, unintended consequences, and intentional pressures yielded multiple, constant changes in society and organizations (Kling and Star, 1997).

There was continued interest in this period in organizational contexts, focusing on efficiency (Kling and Lamb, 1996), management (Kling and Tilquist, 1998), organizational politics (Kling and Lamb, 1999), and values (Kling, 1999). Understanding management and control mechanisms allowed researchers to identify whether directed changes can be coordinated with existing patterns of authority and information and influence flows (Kling and Tilquist, 1998). Mismatches between top down-controls and bottom-up cultures during implementation lead to failure (Kling and Tilquist, 1998), largely because of inefficiency, resistance, and lack of sustainability (Kling and Lamb, 1996). Social and organizational preferences and interests shaped political dynamics surrounding resistance or amenability toward change, as well (Kling and Lamb, 1999). The imbalances between the strength of preferences and the interests of stakeholders represented gradients of values, which can be very hard to overcome, even when they are extremely inequitable (Kling, 1999).

Kling's focus on social values and resultant inequalities of political choices, led to the introduction of a new focus on concepts such as access (Kling, 1998; 1999), infrastructure (Kling, 1999; Kling and Lamb, 1999; Kling and Star, 1997; Lamb, 1996), and the Internet (Kling, 1999; Kling and Lamb, 1996; Kling et al., 1998). Imbalances between preferences and interests lead to access problems in society at large without equal infrastructure to support Internet access (Kling, 1999) and between organizations and the public as new and important technologies are often expensive and, in many cases, the businesses that introduce them control access to them (Kling, 1998). ICTs can be immense in scale, and therefore require complex and costly infrastructure (Kling and Star, 1997; Lamb, 1996). The expense of infrastructure to support the Internet and e-business was also considered by Kling and Lamb (1999), as they sought to understand why narratives about cost-cutting through online business models failed to be persuasive (Kling and Lamb, 1996; 1999). Kling et al. (1998) went on to discuss the role of infrastructure in connecting micro-level ICT issues in use to macro-level ICT issues, including economic and social contexts.

Consequences (Kling and Lamb, 1996; Kling and Star, 1997), constraints (Kling and Tilquist, 1998), and ICT (Kling, 1994; 1996; Kling and Star, 1997; Kling and Tilquist, 1998; Kling et al., 1998; Lamb, 1996) developed into identified concepts, rather than as themes of discussion. It was significant to analyze consequences and constraints in their own right, rather than as acknowledged but unexplored variables, just as it was important to begin to understand the embedded social values and norms within ICT, rather than simply looking at their impacts (Kling and Star, 1997; Kling and Tilquist, 1998). Consequences result from implicit, unarticulated aspects of work that go unaccounted for in planning for change (Kling and Star, 1997), as well as from intentional social changes that are non-sustainable and dependent on other dynamic contexts or variables (Kling and Lamb, 1996). Furthermore, the identification of policy, politics, control, and culture in constraining outcomes also facilitates better planning (Kling and Tilquist, 1998).

Researchers also began to examine collaboration (Kling and Lamb, 1999), communication (Kling, 1997; 1999; Kling and Star, 1997; Kling et al., 1998), and community (Kling, 1996; Kling and Lamb, 1996), both from the perspective that they were supported by ICT, and that they included interactions with ICT. Kling and Lamb (1996; 1999) examined online sales and services, as including and being supported by technology, as well as envisioned cyber utopias, arguing that technological mediation of communities or collaborators did not mitigate socio-economic limitations. Communication online or through technology was shaped by social practice, not wholly technical standards (Kling, 1997; 1999; Kling and Star, 1997; Kling et al., 1998), implying that technologies to support communication and collaboration ought to be human centered (Kling and Star, 1997).

Interest in networks (Kling, 1997; Kling and Lamb, 1999; Lamb, 1996), organizational environments (Contractor and Seibold, 1993), and socio-technical systems (Kling, 1997; Kling and Lamb, 1999) led to the development of these conceptual constructs. This was significant because SI began to characterize situations and contexts as more than a collection of variables, involving systematically formal and informal relationships and interactions; this would later evolve into the socio-technical interaction network (STIN), which was discussed with respect to methods and approaches in both the period of coherence and the transformational period. From this point of view, social reality is structured by policies, infrastructure, informal relationships, and other dynamics that create networks in society (Lamb, 1996) and in organizational environments, where structuration and self-organization constantly shape the environment and interactions (Contractor and Seibold, 1993). Kling described scholarly networks among sociologists and their online scholarly resources as socio-technical systems (1997). Kling and Lamb built on that conceptualization to explain the relationships and interactions within the digital economy (1999).

New concepts and variables were considered during this period as additional scholars identified factors relevant to use, context, and outcomes of the adoption of new technologies. Concepts articulated important areas of concern in an accessible way for policy makers, information professionals, and educators to consider, though SI scholarship was not yet as visible as it was to become.

6.3   CONCEPTS FROM THE PERIOD OF COHERENCE

The concepts analyzed with this variety of theories included many of the same constructs as had been present in earlier periods, as well as a new emphasis on coordination (Lamb and Davidson, 2005), cooperation (Ekbia and Kling, 2005), uncertainty (Courtright, 2004), and governance (Agre, 2000a), each of which is fundamentally linked to network theory, economic theory, political theory, information environments, and political theory. The finding that ICTs are socio-technical network systems produced a concept of socio-technical systems (Kling, 2000a; Sawyer and Rosenbaum 2000).

During this period, the analytical focus of SI began to be defined in terms of social and technical change, making the concept of change central to many analyses (Sawyer and Tapia, 2005). The focus on institutional changes led researchers to describe how the introduction of ICT affected social, normative, and cultural structures (Agre, 2000a; Courtright, 2005; Kling and Iacono, 2001), while organizational change dealt with the formal and informal relationships governed by business rules (Hara and Kling, 2002; Kling, 2000a). Examination of socio-technical change deconstructed the mutually shaping interactions between social and technical factors (Allen, 2005; Iacono et al., 2003; Kling and Iacono, 2001), whereas emphasis on social change sought to explain the directional impact of technology (Kling, 2000a; Lamb and Sawyer, 2005).

Context—with specific emphasis on social context (Courtright, 2004; Kling, 2000a; Kling and McKim, 2000; Kling et al., 2005; Mansell, 2005; Sawyer and Eschenfelder, 2002), as opposed to socio-technical, institutional, and organizational variations—continued to be examined (Iacono et al., 2003; Sawyer, 2005), based on the premise that technologies and their users do not exist or interact in isolation. Institutions provide a conceptual construct to bind formal social arrangements, including norms and practices (Agre, 2002; Kling, 2003b; Lamb and Davidson, 2005; Lamb et al., 2003; Lamb and Kling, 2003). The organizational environment provides another contextual environment in which to examine interactions (Agre, 2000b; Allen, 2005; Ekbia and Kling, 2005; Lamb et al., 2003).

These contexts and arrangements of relationships were studied as networks (e.g., Agre, 2000b; Ekbia and Kling, 2005) and communities (e.g., Kling and Courtright, 2003). Attention was also paid to the infrastructure that supports these arrangements (Courtright, 2005; Davenport, 2001; Kling, 2000a).

Within these contexts, interactions were examined as coordination (Lamb and Davidson, 2005), cooperation (Ekbia and Kling, 2005), collaboration (Agre, 2000a; Kling and McKim, 2000; Kling et al., 2003; Lamb and Davidson, 2005), and communication (Hara and Kling, 2002; Kling, 2000a; Kling and McKim, 2000; Kling et al., 2003; Lamb, 2003; Mansell, 2005; Meyer and Kling, 2002; Wood-Harper and Wood, 2005). By examining these interactions, researchers were able to theorize about power relationships (Agre, 2000a; 2002; Ekbia and Kling, 2005), organizational politics (Sawyer and Tapia, 2005), identity (Lamb and Davidson, 2005; Lamb and Kling, 2003), management (Davenport, 2001; Ekbia and Kling, 2005; Hara and Kling, 2002; Kling, 2000a; 2003b; Kling and Hara, 2004; Sawyer and Tapia, 2005), control (Ekbia and Kling, 2005), complexity (Courtright, 2004; Iacono et al., 2003; Kling and Hara, 2004; Kling et al., 2003; Lamb et al., 2003), and dynamics (Courtright, 2004).

Other conceptual concerns included efficiency (Agre, 2000b), values (Allen, 2005; Kling, 2003b; Sawyer, 2005), access (Hara and Kling, 2002; Kling, 2000a; 2000b; Kling and Callahan, 2003), and consequences (Kling and Hara, 2004). Significant attention was paid to theorizing about the Internet during this period (Agre, 2002; Kling, 2001; Kling and Callahan, 2003; Kling and Courtright, 2003; Kling and McKim, 2000; Lamb et al., 2003).

The introduction of additional conceptual constructs with origins in political, economic, and network science was important in broadening the scope of the discussion to larger-scale social issues, in addition to previous focus on specific institutions and organizations. These themes also reflected research trends in other distinct and tangential areas of study, allowing SI discourse to be accessible and easily integrated with more general academic conversations.

6.4   CONCEPTS FROM THE TRANSFORMATIONAL PERIOD

Although what researchers call their SI-like work and the theories that shape their work change considerably and rapidly, they are looking at largely the same concepts. Themes of control (i.e., Davenport and Horton, 2007), complexity (i.e., Contractor et al., 2011; Tapia and Maitland, 2009), and context (Oltmann et al., 2006), specifically social context (Contractor et al., 2011; Davenport and Horton, 2006; 2007), has led researchers to consider and evaluate relationships and interactions that are supported by ICT for coordination, cooperation (Goggins et al., 2011), and collaboration (Contractor, 2009).

Yet the organizational environment (Robbin et al., 2006) is not simply constituted out of interactions between equally powerful actors; many organizational environments are formally structured with actors in management positions (Contractor et al., 2011; Davenport and Horton, 2007) who control priorities, decisions, and access to information and technology (Davenport and Horton, 2007; King et al., 2007). Constraints (Maldonado, et al., 2010; Oltmann et al., 2006) and limits to access are often intentional, yet there are also unanticipated consequences (Robbin, 2007; Robbin and Day, 2006) under conditions of change (Sawyer and Tyworth, 2006). Distributions of power (Davenport and Horton, 2006; Maldonado, et al., 2010; Robbin and Day, 2006) and organizational politics (Maldonado, et al., 2010) are determinant of interests and control within organizations and groups, thereby affecting organizational changes, which are a primary subject of SI concern.

Researchers have examined organizational (Tapia and Maitland, 2009), institutional (Davenport and Horton, 2006; 2007), socio-technical (Goggins et al., 2011; King et al., 2007), and technical (Orlikowski and Iacono, 2008) changes in organizations and communities, in order to understand the complexity (Contractor et al., 2011; King et al., 2007; Rosenbaum and Shachaf, 2010; Tapia and Maitland, 2009) and dynamics (Contractor et al., 2011; Robbin et al., 2006; Rosenbaum and Shachaf, 2010) of socio-technical interactions and systems (Tapia and Maitland, 2009) in context.

ICTs are important to understand in context because of their inherent social, technical, and organizational natures (Contractor et al., 2011; Davenport and Horton, 2006; Day, 2007). Furthermore, they play increasingly significant roles in individuals' lives and in societies, connecting distant and distributed people and resources through the Internet (Contractor, 2009). These connections form networks (Goggins et al., 2011; Sawyer and Tyworth, 2006), which are important to analyze in order to understand how ideas, information, and media spread within distributed organizations and through society.

Organizations and institutions are formally bounded and structured social arrangements that have been analyzed for their economic and governance implications on society, at local and global scales (Davenport and Horton, 2006; 2007; Maldonado, et al., 2010). Communities have been studied as well, though their varied make-ups and levels of formalization have different social implications (Davenport and Horton, 2007; Goggins et al., 2011; Rosenbaum and Shachaf, 2010). Analysis of organizational, institutional, and community contexts of ICT also serves as the foundation for the study of more complex processes and dynamics, including institutionalization (Elliot and Kraemer, 2007; Sawyer and Tapia, 2007), values (Fleischman, 2014; Robbin and Day, 2006; Robbin et al., 2006), identity (Robbin and Day, 2006; Rosenbaum and Shachaf, 2010), and efficiency (Robbin and Day, 2006). As well, culture and multiculturalism are becoming more prominent in SI work (e.g., Sanfilippo and Fichman, 2014; Hara et al., 2010; Shachaf and Hara, 2007; Shachaf, 2008).

The continued use of a shared vocabulary between SI and socio-technical research indicates common contributions and implies that cross-camp discussions are certainly relevant. The coherence of SI can be seen in the fact that the studies consider and papers reference the same works and points of discussion, despite attention being paid in different, albeit decreasing, areas. Thus the differences between SI and socio-technical approaches might not be as sharp as they may appear, perhaps representing different influences and activities rather than strong theoretical differences.

Concept	First Published in SI Literature	References
Context	1984	Blincoe et al., 2012; Contractor, 2009; Contractor et al., 2011; Courtright, 2004; Davenport and Horton, 2006; 2007; Sawyer and Eschenfelder, 2002; Hara and Rosenbaum, 2008; Iacono et al., 2003; Kling, 1996; 1998; 1999; Kling and Iacono, 1984a; Kling and Star, 1997; Kling and Tilquist, 1998; Lamb, 1996; Kling, 2000a; Kling and McKim, 2000; Kling et al., 2005; Oltmann et al., 2006; Robbin and Day, 2006; Robbin et al., 2006; Sawyer, 2005; Sawyer and Tapia, 2005; Tapia and Maitland, 2009
Control	1984	Davenport and Horton, 2007; Ekbia and Kling, 2003; King et al., 2007; Kling and Iacono, 1984a; 1984b; 1989; Maldonado et al., 2010; Robbin and Day, 2006
Institutions	1984	Agre, 2002; Contractor, 2009; Elliot and Kraemer, 2007; Iacono and Kling, 1988; Kling, 2003b; Kling and Iacono, 1984a; 1989; Lamb and Davidson, 2005; Lamb et al., 2003; Lamb and Kling, 2003; Sawyer and Tapia, 2007
Management	1984	Blincoe et al., 2012; Contractor, 2009; Contractor et al., 2011; Davenport, 2001; Davenport and Horton, 2007; Ekbia and Kling, 2003; Hara and Kling, 2002; Kling, 2000a; 2003b; Kling and Hara, 2004; Kling and Iacono, 1984a; 1989; Kling and Tilquist, 1998; Maldonado et al., 2010; Sawyer and Tapia, 2005
Organizational Politics	1984	Kling and Iacono, 1984b; 1989; Kling and Lamb, 1999; Maldonado et al., 2010; Sawyer and Tapia, 2005
Power Relationships	1984	Agre, 2000a; 2002; Davenport and Horton, 2006; Ekbia and Kling, 2003; Kling and Iacono, 1984b; 1989; Maldonado et al., 2010; Robbin and Day, 2006

Table 6.1: Chronology of conceptual development from an SI perspective

Change	1988	Agre, 2000a; Allen, 2005; Contractor and Seibold, 1993; Courtright, 2005; Davenport and Horton, 2006; 2007; Goggins et al., 2011; Hara and Kling, 2002; Iacono, 1996; Iacono et al., 2003; King et al., 2007; Kling, 1994; 1996; 2000a; Kling and Iacono, 1988; 2001; Kling et al., 1998; Kling and Star, 1997; Kling and Tilquist, 1998; Lamb and Sawyer, 2005; Orlikowski and Iacono, 2008; Sawyer and Tyworth, 2006; Tapia and Maitland, 2009
Values	1988	Allen, 2005; Kling, 1999; 2003b; Kling and Iacono, 1988; Robbin and Day, 2006; Robbin et al., 2006; Sawyer, 2005
Complexity	1989	Contractor et al., 2011; Courtright, 2004; Davenport and Horton, 2006; 2007; Iacono et al., 2003; Kling, 1996; 1999; Kling and Hara, 2004; Kling and Iacono, 1989; King et al., 2007; Kling et al., 2003; Kling and Star, 1997; Kling and Tilquist, 1998; Lamb et al., 2003; Maldonado et al., 2010; Robbin and Day, 2006; Rosenbaum and Shachaf, 2010; Tapia and Maitland, 2009
Efficiency	1989	Agre, 2000b; Kling and Iacono, 1989; Kling and Lamb, 1996; Robbin and Day, 2006
Organizational Environments	1993	Agre, 2000b; Allen, 2005; Contractor and Seibold, 1993; Ekbia and Kling, 2005; Lamb et al., 2003; Robbin et al., 2006
ICTs and Information Technology	1994	Agre, 2000a; 2000b; 2002; Contractor et al., 2011; Courtright, 2004; Davenport and Horton, 2006; Day, 2007; Ekbia and Kling, 2003; 2005; Elliot and Kraemer, 2007; Goggins et al., 2011; Hara and Kling, 2002; Hara and Rosenbaum, 2008; Iacono et al., 2003; Kling, 1994; 1996; 2000a; 2000b; Kling and Hara, 2004; Kling et al., 1998; Kling et al., 2005; Kling and Star, 1997; Kling and Tilquist, 1998; Lamb, 1996, 2003; 2005; Lamb and Kling, 2003; Mansell, 2005; Orlikowski and Iacono, 2008; Robbin, 2007; Sawyer, 2005; Sawyer and Eschenfelder, 2002; Sawyer and Tapia, 2006; Wood-Harper and Wood, 2005
Community	1996	Davenport and Horton, 2007; Goggins et al., 2011; Kling, 1996; Kling and Courtright, 2003; Kling and Lamb, 1996; Rosenbaum and Shachaf, 2010
Consequences	1996	Kling and Hara, 2004; Kling and Lamb, 1996; Kling and Star, 1997; Robbin, 2007; Robbin and Day, 2006; Robbin et al., 2006
Infrastructure	1996	Courtright, 2005; Davenport, 2001; Kling, 1999; 2000a; Kling and Lamb, 1999; Kling and Star, 1997; Lamb, 1996

Internet	1996	Agre, 2002; Contractor, 2009; Kling, 1999; 2001; Kling and Callahan, 2003; Kling and Courtright, 2003; Kling and Lamb, 1996; Kling and McKim, 2000; Kling et al., 1998; Lamb et al., 2003
Networks	1996	Agre, 2000a; 2000b; Contractor, 2009; Contractor et al., 2011; Courtright, 2005; Ekbia and Kling, 2005; Goggins et al., 2011; Hara and Kling, 2002; Kling, 1997; 2000a; 2000b; 2001; 2003b; Kling and Lamb, 1999; Kling et al., 2003; Lamb, 1996; 2003; Lamb and Davidson, 2005; Lamb and Kling, 2003; Mansell, 2005; Meyer and Kling, 2002; Sawyer and Tyworth, 2006
Communication	1997	Hara and Kling, 2002; Kling, 1997; 1999; 2000a; Kling and McKim, 2000; Kling et al., 2003; Kling and Star, 1997; Kling et al., 1998; Lamb, 2003; Mansell, 2005; Meyer and Kling, 2002; Wood-Harper and Wood, 2005
Dynamics	1997	Courtright, 2004; Contractor et al., 2011; Kling, 1997; Kling and Star, 1997; Robbin et al., 2006; Rosenbaum and Shachaf, 2010
Human Centered	1997	Kling and Star, 1997
Social practice	1997	Kling, 1997; 1999; Kling et al., 1998; Kling and Star, 1997
Socio-technical Systems	1997	Kling, 1997; 2000a; Kling and Lamb, 1999; Sawyer and Rosenbaum, 2000; Tapia and Maitland, 2009
Access	1998	Hara and Kling, 2002; Kling, 1998; 1999; 2000a; 2000b; Kling and Callahan, 2003; Maldonado et al., 2010; Oltmann et al., 2006
Constraints	1998	Kling and Tilquist, 1998; Maldonado et al., 2010; Oltmann et al., 2006
Collaboration	1999	Agre, 2000a; Contractor, 2009; Goggins et al., 2011; Kling and Lamb, 1999; Kling and McKim, 2000; Kling et al., 2003; Lamb and Davidson, 2005; Maldonado et al., 2010
Governance	2000	Agre, 2000a; Davenport and Horton, 2006; 2007; Maldonado et al., 2010
Identity	2003	Lamb and Davidson, 2005; Lamb and Kling, 2003; Robbin and Day, 2006; Rosenbaum and Shachaf, 2010
Uncertainty	2004	Courtright, 2004
Cooperation	2005	Ekbia and Kling, 2005; Goggins et al., 2011
Coordination	2005	Blincoe et al., 2012; Goggins et al., 2011; Lamb and Davidson, 2005

CHAPTER 7

Topics

Topics refer to the issues studied within SI, ranging from scholarly communication to online communities to information systems.

7.1 TOPICS FROM THE FOUNDATIONAL PERIOD

Foci of early SI work centered on technology (Kling and Iacono, 1984a; 1984b; 1988; 1989) and its uses in business (Kling and Iacono, 1984a; 1984b; 1988; 1989) and education (Kling and Iacono, 1988). Specifically, researchers studied computerization (Kling and Iacono, 1984a; 1984b; 1988), education and learning (Kling and Iacono, 1988), information systems (Kling and Iacono, 1984b; 1988; 1989), and ICT in the workplace and in diverse organizational contexts (Kling and Iacono, 1984a; 1989).

Computerization had been previously considered from technical perspectives; analysis of the social aspects of computing, a central premise in SI, was an innovative and critical advance made by Kling and his colleagues (Kling and Iacono, 1984a; 1984b; 1988). Computerization in education represented a specific movement, driven by optimism that technology would revolutionize teaching and learning, so as to enable students to be prepared for a different economy and experience transformative social equity, which never happened (Kling and Iacono, 1988).

Interest in characterizing information systems stemmed from their increasingly pervasive use with highly variable outcomes (Kling and Iacono, 1989). These systems were adopted and integrated into existing institutions and organizations, ranging from government bureaucracies to schools to businesses and into homes. Information systems were often adopted with inaccurate understandings and unreasonable expectations, which Kling and Iacono sought to deconstruct and dispel (1984b; 1988). There had also been relatively little attention paid to the post-implementation developments of information systems, including systems abandonment, prior to this time (Kling and Iacono, 1984b). Organizational contexts of ICT use were significant to many workers, across organizations, institutions, units, space, and time (Kling and Iacono, 1984a; 1989).

These early studies illustrated the viability and public significance of a new approach to understanding social problems surrounding technology in context, as well as provided a foundation for more diverse analyses of these and related topics in the future.

7.2   TOPICS FROM THE PERIOD OF EXPANSION

Just as units and concepts of interest diversified and expanded in scope, so too did the topics of analysis. During this period of expansion, computerization (Iacono, 1996; Kling, 1994; 1996; 1998; 1999; Kling and Star, 1997) and a narrow focus on information systems (Contractor and Seibold, 1993; Kling, 1998; Kling and Lamb, 1999; Kling and Star, 1997; Lamb, 1996), while continuing to be considered, did not wholly capture the focus of SI perspectives.

SI research provided a more nuanced view of ICT implementation and computerization in business environments, explaining why outcomes were not as had been anticipated (Kling, 1996). Organizational and workplace cases (Contractor and Seibold, 1993; Kling, 1996; Kling and Lamb, 1999) now dovetailed with interests in business process re-engineering (Kling and Tilquist, 1998). The trend within the popular and trade literature to promote technology as the only legitimate road to increased performance, productivity, and continued viability was reminiscent of earlier deterministic narratives rejected by Kling and colleagues (Kling and Tilquist, 1998). Promotion of technology without really understanding the context into which it was being inserted led to unrealized expectations of positive organizational transformation (Contractor and Seibold, 1993), as well as negative changes and implementation failures, due to unsustainable and non-symbiotic configurations (Kling and Lamb, 1996).

Education and learning research (Iacono, 1996) complemented and provided a bridge to applying SI perspectives to scholarly communication (Kling, 1997). The Internet and increasing computerization in society led to changes in social priorities surrounding the role of information technology in learning (Iacono, 1996), education, and academia (Kling, 1997). Some of these changes happened gradually and unintentionally as an information society developed (Iacono, 1996), while others were planned; Kling specifically described how minor changes had occurred for scholars in sociology and prescribed how the Internet could be used to support communication, professional networks, and intellectual debate among sociologists (1997).

Along with a developing awareness of an information society (Iacono, 1996; Kling, 1998), computer-mediated communication (Kling, 1994), online communities (Kling and Lamb, 1996), policy (Kling, 1996), and design (Kling, 1996; Kling and Star, 1997) issues began to occupy SI scholars throughout the 1990s. The impact of the Internet and its pervasive use and application led to new interests in socio-technical relationships; Kling was particularly interested in how communities and communication were supported by the Internet and could be facilitated through design and policy (Kling, 1994;1996; Kling and Lamb, 1996). The idea of social computerization (Kling, 1996) and a new information society (Iacono, 1996; Kling, 1998) led to critical analyses of planned online communities as cyber-utopias (Kling and Lamb, 1996) and human-centered information systems (Kling and Star, 1997), which was significant because these researchers found that technology was so closely tied to social structure and use that new technologies alone were not sufficient to provide social justice or redistribute power (Iacono, 1996; Kling, 1998; Kling and Star, 1997).

In applying interdisciplinary SI approaches to more diverse topics, the significance of SI to problem solving in a society that was becoming increasingly computerized became more evident. Topical and domain diversity strengthened SI by increasing relevance and reshaping discussions in a variety of domains.

7.3   TOPICS FROM THE PERIOD OF COHERENCE

Topics of interest in SI were largely carried over from early work through this period, though SI principles were newly applied during this period to information behavior (Allen, 2005; Courtright, 2005; Lamb et al., 2003; Lamb and Kling, 2003), knowledge and information management (Davenport, 2001; Ekbia and Kling, 2003; Hara and Kling, 2002; Kling, 2000a; 2003b; Kling and Hara, 2004), libraries (Kling, 2001), and communities of practice (Davenport, 2001; Hara and Kling, 2002; Kling and Courtright, 2003).

Studies of communities of practice tended to correlate with and complement research on education and learning (Agre, 2000a; 2000b; Davenport, 2001; Hara and Kling, 2002; Kling and Hara, 2004), ICT in the workplace (Davenport, 2000; 2005; Iacono et al., 2003; Lamb et al., 2003; Sawyer and Eschenfelder, 2002), and online communities (Davenport, 2001; Hara and Kling, 2002; Kling and Courtright, 2003). Similar areas of research included continued emphasis on computer-mediated communication (Hara and Kling, 2002; Kling and McKim, 2000) and scholarly communication (Kling and Callahan, 2003; Kling and McKim, 2000; Kling et al., 2003; Meyer and Kling, 2002).

The focus on computerization (Iacono et al., 2003; Kling, 2000a; 2000b; 2001; Kling and Iacono, 2001) and information systems (Allen, 2005; Iacono et al., 2003; Wood-Harper and Wood, 2005) within an information society persisted. There was strong interest in applying findings to policy (Agre, 2000a; 2002; Iacono et al., 2003; Lamb et al., 2003) and design solutions (Kling, 2003b; Kling et al., 2005; Sawyer, 2005; Sawyer and Tapia, 2005), representing the normative orientation of SI, which was associated with business process re-engineering (Sawyer and Tapia, 2005).

Broad subject interests reflected the research agendas of new participants, as well as influenced increased theoretical breadth. The depth of study of some topics that had received earlier SI attention was also significant in yielding new findings and conclusions. The topics considered also reflected Kling's interests; attention toward computerization during this period, for example, was largely in acknowledging Kling's contributions to SI, rather than providing new insights.

7.4   TOPICS FROM THE TRANSFORMATIONAL PERIOD

Topics considered in recent years have seemingly narrowed, with scholarship converging around online (e.g., Goggins et al., 2011) and workplace technology issues (e.g., Contractor et al., 2011), as well as normative implications for policy (Oltmann et al., 2006) and design (Blincoe et al., 2012). Within these contexts, research has shown a revitalized focus on computerization (e.g., Hara and Rosenbaum, 2008), which seemingly was disappearing from use in empirical work through the early 2000s, for example with Allen's (2005) application of Kling's conceptualization of computerization, which did not use the word computerization in discussing data around enterprise systems, after the initial introduction of theory within the published work.

With regard to organizations and ICT in the workplace, many have explored this topic generally (e.g., Sawyer and Tapia, 2006; Tapia and Maitland, 2009). However, some researchers were concerned more specifically with knowledge and information management (e.g., Davenport and Horton, 2007; Maldonado et al., 2010) or information systems (e.g., Sawyer and Tyworth, 2006).

In online contexts, online communities and virtual teams have received substantial attention (e.g., Goggins et al., 2011; Rosenbaum and Shachaf, 2010; Shachaf and Hara, 2007). In both online and organizational contexts, the study of communities of practice has sought to understand how situated learning and information sharing is coordinated through engagement within particular groups (Goggins et al., 2011; Rosenbaum and Shachaf, 2010).

The practical implications of SI are seemingly resurgent, with an emphasis on solving social problems surrounding technology and finding better technical solutions for social contexts. There have been efforts to make SI benefit public interests and relevant for policy and decision-makers. For example, Tapia et al. (2011) examined policy driven initiatives, as institutional efforts, directed at shaping and altering socio-technical systems for the public good. Their study provided insights on how values and ideological interests impact ICT configurations and social outcomes, so as to support the development of more informed initiatives in future efforts.

CHAPTER 8

Findings

Findings from seminal SI works are described; exploring them throughout the four stages makes it apparent that over time some repeatable findings unify SI scholarship. A chronology of findings and key references supporting these assertions is provided in Table 8.1, following details of the development of key findings throughout each period. Table 8.2 provides examples of support from the literature for these findings.

8.1   FINDINGS FROM THE FOUNDATIONAL PERIOD

In this foundational stage, SI findings were iterated as descriptive accounts of the reality of computerization in organizations, rather than as prescriptive and technologically optimistic computerization goals. Kling and Iacono found that:

1. Politics and interests impact ICT outcomes (1984b; 1988; 1989);

2. ICT use is situated and context dependent (1988; 1989);

3. Context is complex (1984a);

4. ICTs favor the status quo (1984a; 1984b);

5. ICTs are not value neutral (1988); and

6. ICTs have multiple and paradoxical impacts (1989).

These findings explained not only why popular discourses about and expectations for positive impacts of technology on organizations were often problematic, but also why future assessment and theorization needed to be contextual and to consider a spectrum of social and technological details (Kling and Iacono, 1984a; 1989).

The complexity of control in institutional computerized work contexts revealed that expectations of social change resulting from new technologies were often unrealistic (Kling and Iacono, 1984a). Case studies of information systems adoption revealed that it was unlikely that a consequence would be changes in organizational structure and power because key actors leveraged authority and influence to gain legitimacy, encouraging computerization because it was in their own self-interest (Kling and Iacono, 1984b). Thus, strategic and political interests were found to have significant impacts on computing outcomes from pre- to post-implementation of information systems (Kling and Iacono, 1984b; 1988; 1989).

Interests impacting opinions in computerization movements, as initiatives that promote new technologies or new uses of technology, are representative of values placed on the power of computing and social change by participants in debates about computing (Kling and Iacono, 1988). These values, which often lead to activism for computerization, are falsely grounded in the belief that people are the problem when computerization fails to meet expectations, because in reality the technology was not fitting into the specific context (Kling and Iacono, 1988). The empirical evidence shows that the design and implementation of ICTs are socio-technical activities, and therefore coordinating ICT with organizational structure and meeting the technical needs of a group or organization are crucial (Kling and Iacono, 1988; 1989). Because use is situated and contexts vary, particular socio-technical interactions lead to different, and sometimes contradictory, outcomes (Kling and Iacono, 1989). To summarize, Kling and Iacono (1984a; 1984b; 1988; 1989) provided empirical support for the argument that ICTs are not used in vacuums and cannot be isolated from the socio-technical and organizational variables surrounding their use when planning for, designing, implementing, and using them.

8.2   FINDINGS FROM THE PERIOD OF EXPANSION

The shared, repeatable findings common to SI research have long been one of its unifying features. Significant work throughout the 1990s further supported early conclusions that: ICTs are not value neutral (Kling, 1996), context is significant and complex (Kling, 1998; Kling and Star 1997; Kling and Tilquist, 1998), politics and strategic interests impact outcomes of ICT design and use (Kling and Lamb, 1996), ICTs tend to reinforce the status quo (Contractor and Seibold, 1993; Kling, 1999; Kling and Tilquist, 1998), and ICT use is situated and context dependent (Iacono, 1996). However, additional conclusions were developed, including:

1. Context impacts implementation and use (Contractor and Seibold, 1993; Kling, 1996; 1998; Kling and Lamb, 1999; Kling and Tilquist, 1998; Lamb, 1996);

2. Social shaping and context of technology matter (Iacono, 1996; Kling, 1998; 1999; Kling and Star 1997);

3. Change is constant (Kling, 1996);

4. There are unintended consequences of ICT design and use (Kling and Lamb, 1996);

5. There is a productivity paradox associated with ICT (Kling, 1998; Kling and Star 1997);

6. Outcome distributions are unequal (Kling, 1999; Kling and Star 1997);

7. There are moral and ethical aspects of ICT (Kling, 1996);

8. Articulation is important (Kling, 1999; Kling and Lamb, 1999);

9. External factors affect interaction (Kling and Lamb, 1996);

10. ICT users are social actors (Iacono, 1996); and

11. Incentives matter (Kling and Lamb, 1999).

These findings illustrated the nuances of analyzing social and technical interaction in context.

While earlier research had emphasized that use of technology does not happen in a vacuum and the situated nature of ICT is important, how context specifically affected ICT in stages of implementation and use had not been explored (Kling, 1996). Context was now found to strongly impact implementation and use because of (1) the preferences of individuals in decision making (Kling and Lamb, 1999), and (2) the practices and habits of users, which determine ICT implementation and use in organizations (Kling, 1996). This impact, empirically assessed, better explained why outcomes varied across contexts because the complexity of work environments and processes is specific and does not fit perfectly into general systems and technologies (Kling, 1998). Contractor and Seibold (1993) identified the impact of user experience and communication between users in context as deteminants of outcomes, and Lamb (1996) further explored the ways in which other social interactions and relationships impacted outcomes. Social context (Contractor and Seibold, 1993; Lamb, 1996) and cultural models determine change, implementation, and use of ICT (Kling and Tilquist, 1998).

This concept of the social context and the subsequent social shaping of technology framework are important because the meaning and value of technologies are socially constructed by the groups and organizations who use them (Iacono, 1996); in addition, these groups have been shaped by sociopolitical and historical factors, creating ideologies, and defining their habits and practices (Iacono, 1996). In this sense, all groups are not equal and social discrepancies and disparities greatly impact computerization and public access (Kling, 1998; 1999). This social embeddedness of technology determines outcomes, negative externalities, changes, and consequences (Kling and Star 1997). Social factors are important because users of technologies are social actors who create social dynamics, institutions, norms, and practices (Iacono, 1996).

It is important to recognize that unequal outcomes of ICT use result in part from the unequal social origins of users and from advantaged and disadvantaged actors, making the potential for social justice through technological change or innovation alone extremely unlikely (Kling and Star 1997). Assumptions that advanced technology will provide improvement fail to recognize the importance of access issues and thus unintended outcomes and consequences are experienced because the situation was not as simple and equitable as assumed (Kling, 1998). Unintended consequences, negative externalities, and lack of sustainability lead to technological failure because socio-economic embeddedness limits the extent to which people using ICT and online environments can create their envisioned utopias (Kling and Lamb, 1996). Inequality and consequences of ICT imply that there are winners and losers, meaning that ICTs have moral and ethical qualities (Kling, 1996).

In addition to complex contexts, change is constant in reality. Kling (1996) discussed the dynamics of computerization in terms of human changes, control and privacy changes, risks of accidents or failures, and the constant evolution of work practices that change the context of ICT as time passes. Change also results from other changes; when new technologies are introduced, they affect work and social practices and implicit processes are often challenged or overlooked in this process (Kling, 1999; Kling and Lamb, 1999). Articulation work is extremely important to predict, control, and minimize negative consequences and ensures that systems do not over-simplify the processes they are designed to emulate or support (Kling, 1999) by making the implicit explicit (Kling and Lamb, 1999).

Yet, it is not only the unnoticed within organizations that affects outcomes; external factors play a role, including interaction with regulatory agencies, clients' or partners' needs, and industry-wide changes (Kling and Lamb, 1999). In adopting technologies, organizations largely hope to increase productivity, but sometimes find that automation investments and actual gains are paradoxical (Kling and Star, 1997). Increases in productivity do not keep pace with the cost of technologies (Kling, 1998), therefore incentives really do matter in encouraging users to learn to use the technology to optimal levels (Kling and Lamb, 1999).

These findings indicate there are many more facets to socio-technical interactions than values (Kling, 1996), power balances (Contractor and Seibold, 1993), and situatedness (Iacono, 1996), which were previously evaluated. Findings of SI research in this period begin to explain more precisely and under different conditions what the role of ICT is in social and organizational change.

8.3   FINDINGS FROM THE PERIOD OF COHERENCE

Many earlier findings were reinforced and further supported in new contexts during this period. Findings were further verified surrounding the social context; for example, there is social shaping and a socio-technical context of technology (e.g., Kling, 2000a; 2000b; Kling et al., 2005), context impacts ICT implementation and use (e.g., Kling, 2001; 2003b), and ICT use is situated and context dependent (e.g., Kling et al., 2003; Kling, 1996; Sawyer and Rosenbaum, 2000). These findings mutually reinforce SI principles and support conclusions about the significance of analyzing social and contextual variables as they situate and interact with ICT.

Agre's (2000a) analysis of higher education and challenges to arguments that the technological infrastructure will fundamentally change universities as institutions showed that the context of technology is social, as well as that this context impacts technologies. Empirical evidence simply does not support the claim that introducing new technologies will force institutions to completely standardize and reform their practices (Agre, 2000a; Hara and Kling, 2002; Sawyer and Tapia, 2005), because the complexity of context matters (Courtright, 2004; Kling, 2001; Kling et al., 2005). Kling and McKim (2000) explained how even the social norms and forces of different scholarly domains provided different stabilizing and destabilizing factors with respect to technological media.

Evidence reveals that context impacts attitudes toward technology and its implementation, adoption, and use (Davenport, 2005; Kling, 2001; 2003b; Kling and Hara, 2004). Kling and Hara (2004) explained how context shapes the implementation of technology in education and how consequences arise from this context. Davenport (2005) argued that this evidence supports a foundational principle of SI; when technologies are implemented, their use cannot be separated from their contexts (Kling and Iacono, 2001; Lamb and Davidson, 2005; Lamb et al., 2003; Lamb and Kling, 2003; Lamb and Sawyer, 2005; Meyer and Kling, 2002; Sawyer, 2005). In order to understand changes that result from and unanticipated results experienced through ICT use, the situation, environment, and social aspects of users must be considered (Davenport, 2005; Kling, 2003b; Kling and McKim, 2000; Mansell, 2005; Sawyer and Eschenfelder, 2002; Wood-Harper and Wood, 2005).

These diverse factors, along with the particular histories of organizations and individuals, and the structures within which they operate create highly complex contexts (e.g., Kling, 2000b; Kling et al., 2005; Lamb and Sawyer, 2005; Sawyer, 2005). Research continued to indicate that simplistic analyses in planning for technological change often led to unintended consequences and negative externalities because reality was more complex (Courtright, 2004). For example, the role of multiple incentives and practices competing and interacting in these contexts would often be overlooked, leading to analyses that missed significant factors influencing outcomes (Ekbia and Kling, 2005; Kling et al., 2003; Lamb et al., 2003). Findings also revealed that subtle differences in context impact outcomes in complex ways (Mansell, 2005), such as normative differences between and within scholarly domains (Kling, 2003b; Kling and Callahan, 2003; Meyer and Kling, 2002). Wood-Harper and Wood presented an approach for information system planning that emphasizes consideration of multiple perspectives, in order to better account for complexity in context (2005). Within these complex socio-technical contexts, change is constant (Sawyer and Rosenbaum, 2000).

As a result of this complexity, other findings recur, such as the paradoxical impacts of ICT (e.g., Lamb and Sawyer, 2005; Sawyer, 2005; Sawyer and Eschenfelder, 2002; Sawyer and Rosenbaum, 2000), the unintended consequences of ICT use and change (e.g., Courtright, 2004; Davenport, 2005), and the unequal distribution of changes in organizations (e.g., Kling, 2000a; 2000b; Lamb and Sawyer, 2005; Sawyer, 2005; Sawyer and Eschenfelder, 2002; Sawyer and Rosenbaum, 2000). Agre, for example, found that business and political governance narratives about technology painted idealized views of the positive impact of ICT on those spheres, yet analyses provided detailed evidence of countervailing factors, consequences, and inequalities, rather than standardization (2000b; 2002). Expectations founded in inaccurate assumptions lead to unexpected situations in which investments made exceed productivity gains or exacerbate inequalities (Kling and Hara, 2004; Meyer and Kling, 2002). Furthermore, there is evidence that when information professionals don't understand the complexity of their organizations, ICTs are used in unplanned ways (Kling, 2003b; Kling and Hara, 2004).

Lamb and Sawyer (2005) asserted that many of those recurring findings associated with the impact of complexity on computerization outcomes are in fact "common knowledge." They specifically articulated that

> A particular ICT's impacts are rarely isolated to a desired area, but rather are spread to a much larger number of people through the socio-technical links that comprise context. An examination of the larger context often reveals multiple effects, rather than one all – encompassing outcome, and unexpected as well as planned events (p. 16).

In this sense, unequal and unanticipated outcomes from the introduction or use of technologies created new problems beyond those that were being addressed by changes in the socio-technical system in the first place, leading to a paradox in the use of ICTs. Evaluation of ICTs was found to be complex because expected benefits may be outweighed by unexpected consequences, yet it is difficult to account for the consequences given their surprising and distributed nature.

Some iterated SI findings emphasize particular aspects of the complex context that lead to surprising outcomes; planning often accounts for the technical requirements, but too often ignores cultural or institutional aspects. For example, politics and strategic interests impact outcomes (e.g., Agre, 2002; Allen, 2005; Lamb et al., 2003; Mansell, 2005; Wood-Harper and Wood, 2005), and external factors affect interactions between users, technologies, and context (Courtright, 2005; Ekbia and Kling, 2005; Kling, 2001; Kling and Courtright, 2003; Kling et al., 2003; Lamb et al., 2003).

Politics, preferences, and a permeable environment are important in influencing outcomes because ICT users are social actors who interact with other contexts and with each other (Davenport, 2001; Kling, 2000b; Kling et al., 2003; Kling et al., 2005; Lamb et al., 2003; Lamb and Kling, 2003; Wood-Harper and Wood, 2005). ICTs are not value neutral, despite the fact that they are frequently conceptualized as sterile, standardized tools; users, designers, and supportive infrastructures embed values within ICTs and within the use of ICTs (Kling and Courtright, 2003; Kling et al., 2005; Lamb and Sawyer, 2005; Meyer and Kling, 2002; Sawyer, 2005; Sawyer and Eschenfelder, 2002; Sawyer and Rosenbaum, 2000). The recurring patterns within SI findings support a nuanced and sound perspective from which to challenge arguments based on non-empirical premises; as well, continued empirical support for these findings strengthened SI during this period.

However, some premises began to be challenged in subtle ways (Agre, 2002), leading to debate among SI scholars over whether or not ICTs favor the status quo (Agre, 2002; Davenport,

2000; Ekbia and Kling, 2003; Meyer and Kling, 2002; Sawyer and Rosenbaum, 2000). Continued critical analysis also revealed evidence to support new findings, including:

1. ICTs and their contexts are mutually shaping (Agre, 2000a; 2000b; Hara and Kling, 2002; Kling, 2001; Kling et al., 2005; Lamb and Sawyer, 2005; Sawyer, 2005; Sawyer and Eschenfelder, 2002; Sawyer and Rosenbaum, 2000);

2. Technology affects professional identity (Hara and Kling, 2002; Lamb and Davidson, 2005);

3. ICTs are socio-technical network systems (Kling, 2000a; 2000b; Kling and Iacono, 2001; Kling et al., 2003; Lamb and Kling, 2003; Lamb and Sawyer, 2005);

4. ICTs are configurable (Kling et al., 2003; Kling et al., 2005); and

5. ICTs have social, technical, and institutional natures (Kling et al., 2005; Lamb and Sawyer, 2005; Sawyer, 2005).

These understandings reflect increased specificity and refinement of SI ideas.

Repeated findings indicated that the mutually shaping relationships between ICT and context result from iterated interactions (e.g., Kling, 2001; Kling et al., 2005; Sawyer, 2005; Sawyer and Eschenfelder, 2002; Sawyer and Rosenbaum, 2000). Hara and Kling (2002) provided one example, explaining how as social forces change the context, uses of ICT change, and as new technologies are introduced, social shifts occur. Lamb and Sawyer (2005) presented a version of the socio-technical perspective, which considers interdependencies and networked links over time as shaping both the social and technical interactants in context. In this sense, ICTs are socio-technical network systems (e.g., Kling, 2000a; 2000b; Kling and Iacono, 2001). Scholarly communication forums and scholarly norms, for example, structure professional networks for discussion and collaboration through technologically mediated channels (Kling et al., 2003). Lamb and Kling (2003) conceptualize the social interactions between people and technologies as a network dependent on users as social actors with affiliations, environments, interactions, and identities.

In this sense, ICTs have social, technical, and institutional natures (Kling et al., 2005; Lamb and Sawyer, 2005; Sawyer, 2005). The social nature of ICT is manifested in the ways in which these technologies are interpreted and used differently by different people, enable and constrain social actions and relationships, provide means to alter control structures and have negative consequences for some stakeholders (Kling et al., 2005). The technical nature includes communicative and computational roles, temporal and spatial consequences, rare instances of social transformation, and an inability of ICTs to solve things by themselves (Kling et al., 2005). ICTs have an institutional nature and, like the social and technical consequences of ICT use, are embedded in institutional contexts and political consequences that can reframe institutions (Kling et al., 2005). Until recently, however, many scholars have focused exclusively on the social and institutional natures or contexts (Lamb and Sawyer, 2005), leaving attention to the technical nature of ICT underdeveloped.

Focusing on the technical nature, empirical evidence supports the claim that ICTs are configurable (Kling et al., 2003; Kling et al., 2005). Technology is embedded in cultural and institutional contexts, meaning that configurations are dependent on users and regimes of control (Kling et al., 2005). Kling et al. (2003) emphasized the configurability of ICT as fundamental to STIN, with configurations determined by control, dependencies, and governance.

The interaction between the social and technical natures of ICT affects the professional identity of users in organizational contexts (Hara and Kling, 2002; Lamb and Davidson, 2005). Hara and Kling (2002), in studying professional communities of practice, found that less experienced attorneys relied more on ICT because they were less integrated into the community which was bound in part by collective knowledge building and shared identity; the implication is that, in this context, ICT integration is negatively correlated with strong communities of practice (Hara and Kling, 2002). In contrast, Lamb and Davidson (2005) found, in their study at the University of Hawaii, that ICT enhanced scientific identities by allowing scientists with specializations or expertise to make greater, more meaningful contributions. While the impacts differed by context, ICT did alter existing identities within professional communities through interactions with attributes associated with expertise and experience. Both studies focused on communities in which experience and expertise served as social capital, yet the introduction of ICTs into these contexts has opposite effects. In the case of the public defenders' office, new attorneys leveraged ICTs for professionalization, thereby compensating for inequalities in status, whereas in the case of scientific collaboratories, ICTs enhanced the status quo (Hara and Kling, 2002).

The introduction of new conclusions and findings augmented the set of explanations available to SI scholars, but perhaps more significantly there was internal debate surrounding the issue of ICT enforcement of the status quo. The tension was important because it indicated a self-critical turn within SI. Expansion and refinement of the central tenets and assertions of SI signified its status as a diverse and active area of scholarship.

8.4   FINDINGS FROM THE TRANSFORMATIONAL PERIOD

SI research during this period has verified in many instances the set of past findings, with some notable exceptions where there have been new claims:

1. The identification of five conceptualizations of ICT as a tool, an ensemble, a proxy, as computational, and as nominal (Orlikowski and Iacono, 2008).

2. ICT shapes social identity by altering belongingness to communities (Wade, 2014; Rosenbaum and Shachaf, 2010).

3. STIN is a useful approach to study socio technical phenomena (Meyer, 2006; 2014; Shachaf and Rosenbaum, 2009; Walker and Creanor, 2009).

4. There are four patterns of bi-directional relationships between ICT and the socio-cultural construct (Sanfilippo and Fichman, 2014).

Some earlier findings faded in popularity during this period, such as the impact of technology on professional identity, which received relatively scant attention (e.g., Hara et al., 2009). The departure from the analysis of professional identity as impacted by technology is particularly interesting given the attention to social identity during this period from social constructivists (i.e., Wade, 2014).

Analysis of social aspects and social change associated with ICT has continued to be a major focus. Analysis of data has continued to indicate and further elucidate the socially shaped nature and context of technology (King et al., 2007; Maldonado et al., 2010; Shachaf and Hara, 2007; Shachaf, 2008). King et al. (2007) specifically emphasized the limitations of rational and critical approaches in predicting social outcomes surrounding computing, particularly with respect to social computing in comparison to professional or scholarly computing, because social forces and viral trends can overwhelm critical perspectives. Furthermore, separations and barriers between users, as social context, are often reinforced in technological collaboration, allowing social factors to shape technical potential (Maldonado et al., 2010).

Research continues to emphasize that ICT users are social actors (Blincoe et al., 2012; Contractor, 2009; Goggins et al., 2011; Rosenbaum and Shachaf, 2010; Shachaf and Hara, 2007) and that ICT comprise socio-technical network systems (Blincoe et al., 2012; Contractor, 2009; Contractor et al. 2011; Goggins et al., 2011; Orlikowski and Iacono, 2008; Singh, 2013).

Emphasis on social dynamics, including political interests and personal preferences (Davenport and Horton, 2006; Maldonado et al., 2010; Robbin and Day, 2006; Robbin et al., 2006; Shachaf and Hara, 2007), has continued to describe, in significant ways, unequal impacts and consequences of social change (Sawyer and Tapia, 2006; Sawyer and Tywroth, 2006; Tapia and Maitland, 2009; Wade, 2014) and explain why in many instances ICT reifies the status quo (Robbin et al., 2006), as those in power advocate what will benefit them.

Yet while there are sometimes predictable patterns about who will benefit from the adoption of new technologies, there are certainly paradoxical impacts of ICT (Oltmann et al., 2006; Sawyer and Tywroth, 2006), in part because:

1. ICTs are not value neutral (Davenport and Horton, 2006; Robbin and Day, 2006; Robbin et al., 2006; Stillman and Linger, 2009);

2. There are moral and ethical aspects of ICT (Davenport and Horton, 2006; Sanfilippo and Fichman, 2014; Robbin et al., 2006; Sawyer and Tywroth, 2006; Shachaf et al., 2008);

3. Contexts are complex (Contractor et al. 2011; Davenport and Horton, 2006; 2007; Hara and Rosenbaum, 2008; Oltmann et al., 2006; Robbin et al., 2006; Rosenbaum and Shachaf, 2010; Sawyer and Tapia, 2006; Shachaf, 2008; Shachaf and Hara, 2007; Tapia and Maitland, 2009); and

4. Contexts impact implementation and use (Davenport and Horton, 2006; 2007; King et al., 2007; Maldonado et al., 2010; Oltmann et al., 2006; Robbin et al., 2006; Sawyer and Tywroth, 2006).

Support for this set of findings within community informatics, particularly in community informatics-supported new urbanism (Shin and Shin, 2012), provides an area of common interest for a tangential group of scholars.

While social variables and dynamics receive considerable attention, context and ICT themselves are at once social, technical, and institutional in nature (Sawyer and Tywroth, 2006). From an institutional perspective, articulation is important because it makes processes and work explicit which may otherwise be overlooked when planning for or implementing new technologies (Contractor et al. 2011; Sawyer and Tapia, 2006), leading to unanticipated consequences.

When social, technical, and institutional complexities interact in context, these factors are mutually shaping (Davenport and Horton, 2006; Robbin et al., 2006). Furthermore, while it may be tempting to analyze factors within a bounded context, the reality is that external factors also affect interaction (Maldonado et al., 2010).

The constricted focus in recent scholarship is consistent with efforts to increase the robustness and validity of SI by pruning topics of discussion with less empirical support or relevance. The collective decrease in the variety of claims may have built upon the glimpse of self-critical debate evident in the early 2000s, and is another important step toward institutionalization.

Table 8.1: Chronology of key findings in SI		
Finding	**First Published**	**References**
Context is complex	1984	Courtright, 2004; Contractor et al. 2011; Davenport and Horton, 2006; 2007; Hara and Rosenbaum, 2008; Kling, 1998; 2001; 2000b; 2003b; Kling and Hara, 2004; Kling and Iacono, 1984a; Kling and Star 1997; Kling and Tilquist, 1998; Kling et al., 2005; Lamb and Sawyer, 2005; Oltmann et al., 2006; Robbin et al., 2006; Rosenbaum and Shachaf, 2010; Sawyer, 2005; Sawyer and Tapia, 2006; Shachaf and Hara, 2007; Tapia and Maitland, 2009; Wood-Harper and Wood, 2005
ICTs favor the status quo	1984	Kling and Iacono, 1984a; 1984b; Contractor and Seibold, 1993; Kling, 1999; Kling and Tilquist, 1998; Agre, 2000a; Hara and Kling, 2002; Sawyer and Tapia, 2005; Agre, 2002; Davenport, 2000; Ekbia and Kling, 2003; Meyer and Kling, 2002; Sawyer and Rosenbaum, 2000; Robbin et al., 2006
Politics and strategic interests impact outcomes	1984	Kling and Iacono, 1984b; 1988; 1989; Kling and Lamb, 1996; Agre, 2002; Allen, 2005; Ekbia and Kling, 2003; 2005; Kling and Callahan, 2003; Kling et al., 2003; Kling et al., 2005; Lamb et al., 2003; Mansell, 2005; Wood-Harper and Wood, 2005; Davenport and Horton, 2006; Maldonado et al., 2010; Robbin and Day, 2006; Robbin et al., 2006; Shachaf and Hara, 2007
ICTs are not value neutral	1988	Kling and Iacono, 1988; Kling, 1996; Kling and Courtright, 2003; Kling et al., 2005; Lamb and Sawyer, 2005; Meyer and Kling, 2002; Sawyer, 2005; Sawyer and Eschenfelder, 2002; Sawyer and Rosenbaum, 2000; Davenport and Horton, 2006; Robbin and Day, 2006; Robbin et al., 2006
ICT use is situated and context dependent	1988	Kling and Iacono, 1988; 1989; Iacono, 1996; Kling et al., 2003; Kling et al., 2005; Sawyer and Rosenbaum, 2000; Davenport, 2005; Kling, 2001; 2003b; Kling and Hara, 2004; Kling and Iacono, 2001; Lamb and Davidson, 2005; Lamb et al., 2003; Lamb and Kling, 2003; Lamb and Sawyer, 2005; Meyer and Kling, 2002; Sawyer, 2005

ICTs have multiple and paradoxical impacts	1989	Kling and Iacono, 1989; Lamb and Sawyer, 2005; Sawyer, 2005; Sawyer and Eschenfelder, 2002; Sawyer and Rosenbaum, 2000; Agre, 2000b; 2002; Oltmann et al., 2006; Sawyer and Tywroth, 2006
Impact of context on implementation and use	1993	Contractor and Seibold, 1993; Kling, 1996; 1998; Kling and Lamb, 1999; Kling and Tilquist, 1998; Lamb, 1996; Kling, 2001; 2003b; Davenport, 2005; Kling and Hara, 2004; Davenport and Horton, 2006; 2007; King et al., 2007; Maldonado et al., 2010; Oltmann et al., 2006; Robbin et al., 2006; Sawyer and Tywroth, 2006
Social shaping and context of technology	1996	Agre, 2000a; Davenport and Horton, 2006; Iacono, 1996; Kling, 1998; 1999; Kling and Star 1997; Kling, 2000a; 2000b; King et al., 2007; Kling et al., 2005; Maldonado et al., 2010; Robbin and Day, 2006; Robbin et al., 2006; Shachaf and Hara, 2007
ICT users are social actors	1996	Iacono, 1996; Davenport, 2001; Kling, 2000b; Kling et al., 2003; Kling et al., 2005; Lamb et al., 2003; Lamb and Kling, 2003; Wood-Harper and Wood, 2005; Blincoe et al., 2012; Contractor, 2009; Goggins et al., 2011; Rosenbaum and Shachaf, 2010; Shachaf and Hara, 2007
There are moral and ethical aspects of ICTs	1996	Kling, 1996; Davenport and Horton, 2006; Robbin et al., 2006; Sawyer and Tyworth, 2006
Change is constant	1996	Kling, 1996; Sawyer and Rosenbaum, 2000
There are unintended consequences	1996	Kling and Lamb, 1996; Davenport, 2005; Kling, 2001; 2003b; Kling and Hara, 2004; Kling and McKim, 2000; Mansell, 2005; Sawyer and Eschenfelder, 2002; Wood-Harper and Wood, 2005; Courtright, 2004; Meyer and Kling, 2002
External factors affect interaction	1996	Kling and Lamb, 1996; Kling and McKim, 2000; Davenport, 2005; Kling, 2003b; Mansell, 2005; Sawyer and Eschenfelder, 2002; Wood-Harper and Wood, 2005; Courtright, 2005; Ekbia and Kling, 2005; Kling, 2001; Kling and Courtright, 2003; Kling et al., 2003; Lamb et al., 2003; Maldonado et al., 2010

There is a productivity paradox	1997	Kling, 1998; Kling and Star 1997
Outcome distributions are unequal	1997	Kling, 1999; Kling and Star 1997; Mansell, 2005; Kling, 2003b; Kling and Callahan, 2003; Meyer and Kling, 2002; Kling, 2000a; 2000b; Lamb and Sawyer, 2005; Sawyer, 2005; Sawyer and Eschenfelder, 2002; Sawyer and Rosenbaum, 2000; Sawyer and Tapia, 2006; Sawyer and Tyworth, 2006; Tapia and Maitland, 2009
Articulation is important	1999	Kling, 1999; Kling and Lamb, 1999; Kling, 2003b; Kling and Lamb, 1996; Contractor et al., 2011; Sawyer and Tapia, 2006
Incentives matter	1999	Kling and Lamb, 1999; Ekbia and Kling, 2005; Kling et al., 2003; Lamb et al., 2003
ICTs and their context are mutually shaping	2000	Agre, 2000a; 2000b; Hara and Kling, 2002; Kling, 2001; Kling et al., 2005; Lamb and Sawyer, 2005; Sawyer, 2005; Sawyer and Eschenfelder, 2002; Sawyer and Rosenbaum, 2000; Davenport and Horton, 2006; Robbin et al., 2006
ICTs are socio-technical network systems	2000	Kling, 2000a; 2000b; Kling and Iacono, 2001; Kling et al., 2003; Lamb and Kling, 2003; Lamb and Sawyer, 2005; Blincoe et al., 2012; Contractor, 2009; Contractor et al., 2011; Goggins et al., 2011; Orlikowski and Iacono, 2008
Technology affects professional identity	2002	Hara and Kling, 2002; Lamb and Davidson, 2005
ICTs are configurable	2003	Kling et al., 2003; Kling et al., 2005; Robbin et al., 2006
ICTs have social, technical, and institutional natures	2005	Kling et al., 2005; Lamb and Sawyer, 2005; Sawyer, 2005; Sawyer and Tyworth, 2006
Five conceptualizations of information technology as a tool, ensemble, proxy, computational, and nominal	2008	Orlikowski and Iacono, 2008

Table 8.2: Support for Key Findings

Claim	Reference	Empirical Support
Politics and strategic interests impact outcomes	Ekbia and Kling, 2005	In their analysis of multivalent negotiated networks within Enron, Ekbia and Kling (2005) described how concentration of power and coercion between highly decentralized units within the organization led to a dysfunctional internal environment in which ICTs were leveraged to obtain information to support political regimes and organizational level changes often failed because of the competition and animosity between units. In this sense, each unit advocated for itself and the political climate was such that each unit's interests were in conflict with others, leading to a toxic environment within the networked organization.
ICTs are not value neutral	Meyer and Kling, 2002	Social informatics research has long asserted that values are embedded within technologies. Meyer and Kling's (2002) study of arXiv as a scholarly repository provided particular support for the claim that "ICTs are not value neutral" by revealing how cultural preferences and norms, reflecting values regarding collaboration and transparency, within the theoretical physics community were operationalized within the technology, which impacted use by mathematicians and astrophysicists.

ICT use is situated and context dependent	Lamb and Davidson, 2005	A series of studies into ICT-supported collaboration within oceanography and marine biology (e.g., Davidson and Lamb, 2000; Lamb and Davidson, 2005) revealed differences in uses of technologies within different contexts. Not only did time and place, with respect to academia and industry matter, but so too did position and experience. ICTs were embedded within their processes, shaping their identities, impacting collaboration, and dissemination, and enabling their work, yet there were context dependent differences in use based on the situational nature of work and their practices were certainly distinct from other research disciplines (Lamb and Davidson, 2005).
ICTs have multiple and paradoxical impacts	Oltmann et al., 2006	Study of the impacts of the 1996 amendments to the Freedom of Information Act (FOIA), which incorporated electronic access or EFOIA, provide support for the assertion that ICTs have multiple and paradoxical impacts (e.g., Oltmann et al., 2006). Specifically, while electronic access to government documents removed barriers to access for much of the public, allowing access to records from individuals homes without having to visit government repositories or offices, ICTs enabled new barriers to access including making it difficult to measure compliance with availability requirements (Oltmann et al., 2006).

Social shaping and context of technology	Agre, 2000a	Not only are ICTs used in social contexts by social actors, but also social factors shape technology in design, development, and implementation. Agre's (2000a) analysis of the networked university not only illustrates how technologies lead to changes in the environment, but also how social dynamics and characteristics of the university shape technologies in the computerization of education. Social norms about the "relative value of lectures and discussions" lead to technological configurations that mimic offline norms, despite the potential for interactive, modularized, and personalized educational opportunities through ICTs and the evidence that alternatives may be more effective (Agre, 2000a, p. 500).
ICT users are social actors	Shachaf and Hara, 2007	Shachaf and Hara's (2007) study of global virtual teams reveals the impacts of social dimensions of group behavior on media selection in ICT-enabled collaboration. Their work provides one example of empirical studies that have supported the social nature of ICT users as actors, rather than neutral operators of technologies.
Outcome distributions are unequal	Tapia and Maitland, 2009	In a study of the use of PDAs, as exemplar wireless devices, in humanitarian relief operations, Tapia and Maitland (2009) found that those in the middle levels of the aid organizations on site were empowered by the use of the technologies, while those without access to wireless devices were further controlled, thereby redistributing and increasing inequality within the hierarchy. Furthermore outcome distributions were also unequal from site to site, indicating the context dependent nature of outcomes (Tapia and Maitland, 2009).

ICTs and their context are mutually shaping	Davenport and Horton, 2006	Davenport and Horton (2006) reinforced the claim that ICTs and their contexts were mutually shaping in their analysis of e-government in the UK. Specifically, they documented how social, political, and historical characteristics of the UK led to customization of ICTs supporting e-government services, as well as how the ICTs led to overall changes in governmental structure and public services (Davenport and Horton, 2006).
ICTs are socio-technical network systems	Goggins et al., 2011	The conception of ICTs as socio-technical networks, which is often associated with research employing STIN analysis, has also been supported in other social informatics research. Specifically, Goggins et al. (2011) explain online group formation as a socio-technical system, lending additional support to past claims that ICT use is networked, within ties between people, information, and technology.

CHAPTER 9

Conclusion

Understanding seminal SI works and the changes in their themes and designs over time and placing SI into an evolutionary framework allows researchers to more firmly ground their work, provides a strategy for students to integrate themselves into the tradition of SI research and theorizing, and maps a trajectory for development in SI approaches. In this sense, this book seeks to advance the agenda of SI in two ways. First we have identified and described the key concepts, ideas, approaches, and findings that unify SI, so as to frame future research. Second, we have pointed out the key challenges and opportunities throughout the history of SI, providing grounds on which to build on the tradition of exemplary SI scholarship while highlighting anticipated tensions moving forward.

This book also describes the evolution of SI as it has emerged and developed in the academic ecosystem. Using an ecological metaphor, we have argued that SI emerged in six different places in the world in the 1980s and the 1990s and that these developments introduced natural competition that unfolded during the 1990s and into the 21st century. In the process of selection that followed, various factors shaped the evolution of the discipline. Although SI is alive and well in all of these locations, political, technological, and linguistic boundaries hindered the spread of Norwegian, Slovenian, Japanese, and Russian versions of SI. At the same time, technological innovations, particularly the ubiquity of global digital communications networks, on which English was the *lingua franca*, played a major role in the outcome, wherein the version of SI that developed in the U.S., along with collaboration with UK scholars, became the dominant form of SI.

The earliest versions of SI blended social science and informatics approaches, drawing on sociology and psychology to study the relationships between ICT and society in the context of work in complex organizations. Many of the themes that were emphasized and introduced into the academic discourse about computerization and society during the 1980s would become key assumptions and insights of modern SI. For example, in Russian SI, Ursal (1989) argued that the relationship between technology and society was best described as one of mutual shaping. From Japanese SI came the assumption that information and, by implication, ICT, play a fundamental role in the constitution and maintenance of modern societies, which is why social phenomena should be studied from an information perspective. From the UK version of SI came the emphasis on studying technology, organizations, and work practices from a socio-technical perspective that draws heavily on a range of social sciences. Despite having SI emerged in six different locations around the globe, for reasons described above, the North American version of SI has become the most widely known and followed. This version has gone through its own evolution, with stages of foundational development, expansion, coherence, and, currently, transformation.

During the 1980s, the foundational period of SI involved the critical assessment of and challenge to the prevailing deterministic discourse about ICT in organizations, and the introduction by SI scholars of a socio-technical approach that made use of empirically grounded concepts of economic rationality, the embeddedness of information systems, and metaphors of organizational politics. The research consistently found that the reality of computerization in organizations was not as it was depicted in the prescriptive and optimistic academic discourse of the time, especially with respect to the claims about the positive implications of social change that were expected to follow from the implementation and use of information technology. The approach taken during this stage was interdisciplinary, making use of institutional shaping, political analysis, computerization movements, and socio-technical thinking, all of which continue to characterize contemporary SI.

This stage was followed by a period of expansion during the 1990s when SI researchers began to pursue more closely aligned research agendas while their findings began to coalesce into a shared core of principles, knowledge, and insights about computerization and society that emphasized the influence of social, cultural, and organizational factors on ICT design, implementation, and use. In terms of the development of SI, this was a period of institutionalization with the establishment of SI research centers, the development of SI curricula in graduate and undergraduate programs, the convening of workshops, and the creation of mini tracks and special interest groups at conferences. Approaches focusing on the importance of the context in which computerization took place that employed critical and socio-technical perspectives began to become more common in SI work at this time.

By the turn of the 21st century and for five years afterward, SI enjoyed a period of coherence, although the seeds of the next and more diverse period were being sown. One critically important activity that unfolded during this time was the sustained growth and development of the core body of SI knowledge, principles, and findings that became a taken-for-granted set of assumptions about ICT, people, work, and context that drove researchers and theorists to engage in the analysis of computerization and society. Chief among these were the continuation of the critical appraisal of and staunch opposition to technological determinism, the use of a socio-technical lens to study computing in social and organizational settings, the development of a normative orientation to the analysis of computerization in society, the explicit concern for the economic and political impacts of ICTs in organizations, and the introduction of the concept of the socio-technical interaction network, a conceptual tool for understanding the complex mutual shaping between people and ICTs in various contexts of use. As well, there was a convergence around a set of assumptions about ICT including their configurability, embeddedness, value-laden nature, and role in shaping positive and negative outcomes for stakeholders. It was this time that the most common and frequently cited definition of SI was proposed by Kling (2000a, 218): "interdisciplinary study of the design, uses, and consequences of ICT that takes into account their interaction with institutional and cultural contexts"; versions of this statement with subtle variations subsequently appeared throughout the

SI literature. By the end of this period, it had become clear that SI had succeeded in reinforcing the core principle that the relationships among ICT, the people who design, implement, manage, and use them, and the contexts of design and use are extremely complex and a challenge for researchers to untangle empirically and theoretically. From the perspective of SI, simplistic discourses about technology and its impacts were woefully inadequate and were to be challenged at every turn.

During the present period of transformation that began in 2006, scholars and researchers, many of whom are new to SI, are expanding its boundaries into new domains and with new theoretical and conceptual lenses. For example, researchers are investigating social phenomena such as group informatics, virtual teams, information inequality, and the social web, and using methods that move beyond focused case studies to larger-scale comparative research. Researchers are moving beyond a simplified notion of ICT to conceptualizations that cast them as a tool, an assemblage, as being embedded in STIN, and as shaping identity in online communities.

This is also a period of increasing institutionalization as SI courses have become part of the undergraduate and graduate curricula at many universities and SI work is well represented at many conferences. Meyer (2014) discusses in greater detail the contours of the intellectual community that has arisen around the core body of knowledge of SI. As of this writing, according to the website "Social Informatics," maintained by the University of Ljubljana, there are ten universities in the U.S. and twenty-three universities and institutes in fourteen countries with programs, doctoral or masters minors, or tracks within degrees focused on SI; there are seven universities that have schools, departments, or faculties of social informatics, all outside the U.S.; and there are many more that offer one or more courses about SI (Vehovar, 2013b). There are research centers, particularly the Rob Kling Center for Social Informatics at Indiana University, that are focal gathering points for researchers interested in SI. Research during this period has revisited the basic principles of SI, including an emphasis on ICT as socio-technical assemblages and the use of a critical perspective. At the same time, many theoretical approaches have been imported from cognate fields to inform SI research.

As the period of transformation further unfolds, SI is poised at a critical point in its development. What does the future look like for SI? In what directions will SI research develop during this decade? What will be its relationships with cognate domains, such as socio-technical analysis, STS, social media studies, human-centered computing, and others?

Following the ecological metaphor, multiple legitimate alternatives for the future of SI are viable. It is possible that North American SI could completely transform, if outcompeted by alternative schools of SI or alternative approaches. Yet this seems unlikely given the growth of SI publications and increasing institutionalization of the discipline. What seems more likely, particularly given the interplay between SI and alternatives, is a continuous slow transformation and expansion of SI.

This transformation could take on many forms, depending in part on the extent of interaction between scholars in associated domains and the relevance of the SI perspective given the nature of questions and paradoxes presented. Specifically, it is likely, for example, that SI and socio-technical disciplines will merge over time, or else differentiate further, so as to provide particular advantages for particular contexts. It is possible that the use of SI as an umbrella term that signifies a collective disciplinary identity will encompass various subdomains in research and teaching and, over time, will contribute to the institutionalization of the discipline.

One interesting trend that illustrates the increasing relevance of SI is that SI researchers are rediscovering, through the critical impulse inherent in SI, the significance and importance of addressing and analyzing social problems with a goal of making recommendations to improve socio-technical assemblages in ways that improve people's lives. This trend is significant because it is part of an ongoing effort to intervene in and affect in positive ways the public discourse about computerization and society. SI researchers are seeking to conduct research that has as an outcome benefiting the public interest and influencing the public policy discourse about people, technology, and work. This leads to speculation about a different type of future for SI, one in which SI researchers and theorists become more deeply engaged in the public discourse about the social and cultural issues of the day that are shaped by developments in technology and computerization.

Bibliography

Adizes, I. 1979. Organizational passages – diagnosing and treating lifecycle problems of organizations. *Organizational Dynamics* 8(1): 3–25. DOI: 10.1016/0090-2616(79)90001-9. 4

Agre, P. E. (2000a). Infrastructure and institutional change in the networked university. *Information, Communication and Society*, 3(4), 494–507. DOI: 10.1080/13691180010002323. 36, 45, 48, 49, 50, 53, 58, 59, 61, 65, 66, 67, 68

Agre, P. (2000b). The market logic of information. *Knowledge, Technology and Policy*, 13(3). 35, 36, 45, 46, 49, 50, 53, 59, 61, 66, 67

Agre, P. E. (2002). Real-time politics: The internet and the political process. *Information Society*, 18(5), 311–331. DOI: 10.1080/01972240290075174. 21, 27, 37, 45, 46, 48, 49, 50, 53, 59, 60, 65

Aldrich, HE. 1999. *Organizations Evolving*. London, UK: Sage Publications.

Allen, J. P. (2005). Value conflicts in enterprise systems. *Information Technology and People*, 18(1), 33–49. DOI: 10.1108/09693840510584612. 29, 37, 45, 46, 49, 53, 54, 60, 65

Aspray, W. (2011). The history of information science and other traditional information domains: Models for future research. *Libraries and the Cultural Record*, 46(2). 230–248. DOI: 10.1353/lac.2011.0011.

Barab, S. A., Kling, R., and Gray, J. H. (2004). *Designing for Virtual Communities in the Service of Learning*. Edited by Sasha A. Barab, Rob Kling, James H. Gray. Cambridge, MA ; New York : Cambridge University Press, 2004. DOI: 10.1017/CBO9780511805080.

Barker, RG. 1968. *Ecological Psychology: Concepts and Methods for Studying the Environment of Human Behavior*. Stanford, California: Stanford University Press. DOI: 10.1126/science.166.3907.856-a.

Blincoe, K., Valetto, G., and Goggins, S. (2012). Proximity. *Libraries and the Cultural RecordComputer Supported Cooperative Work*, 1351. DOI: 10.1145/2145204.2145406. 38, 48, 50, 54, 63, 66, 67

Bronfenbrenner, U. 1979. *The Ecology of Human Development: Experiments by Nature and Design*. Cambridge, Massachusetts: Harvard University Press, 1979.

Bronfenbrenner, U. (1992). *Ecological Systems Theory*. Jessica Kingsley Publishers. 5

Bronfenbrenner, U. and Morris, P. A. (1998). The ecology of developmental processes. *Handbook of Child Psychology*, 1, 993–1028. 5

Brookes, B. C. (1980). "Informatics as the fundamental social science." In: Taylor, Peter J. (ed.). *New Trends in Documentation and Information: Proceedings of the 39th FID Congress*, University of Edinburgh, 25–28 Sept. 1978. FID Publication 566. London: ASLIB. 20

Brookes, B.C. (1984). "Lenin: The founder of informatics." *Journal of Information Science*, 8, 221–223. DOI: 10.1177/016555158400800505.

Burnett, K., Burnett, G., Kazmer, M., Marty, P., Worrall, A., Knop, B., Hinnant, C., Stvilia, B., and Wu, S. (2014). Don't tap on the glass, you'll anger the fish! The information worlds of distributed scientific teams. In P. Fichman, & H. Rosenbaum (Eds.), *Social Pnformatics: Past, Present, and Future* (pp. 1-20). Cambridge, UK: Cambridge Scholars Publishing. 39

Center for Social Informatics. Institute for Informatics and Digital Innovation. Napier University. (2012). About Us https://wiki.inf.ed.ac.uk/Main/SIC. 14

Churchil, NC. and Lewis, VL. 1983. *The Five Stages of Small Business Growth*. Harvard.

Contractor, N. (2009). The emergence of multidimensional networks. *Journal Of Computer-Mediated Communication*, 14(3), 743–747. DOI: 10.1111/j.1083-6101.2009.01465.x. 30, 38, 46, 47, 48, 50, 63, 66, 67

Contractor, N. S., Monge, P. R., and Leonardi, P. M. (2011). Multidimensional networks and the dynamics of sociomateriality: Bringing technology inside the network. *International Journal Of Communication*, 5682–720. 30, 38, 46, 47, 48, 49, 50, 54, 63, 64, 65, 67

Contractor, N. S. and Seibold, D. R. (1993). Theoretical frameworks for the study of structuring processes in group decision support systems. *Human Communication Research*, 19(4), 528. DOI: 10.1111/j.1468-2958.1993.tb00312.x. 21, 26, 27, 34, 35, 42, 44, 49, 52, 56, 57, 58, 65, 66

Courtright, C. (2004). Which lessons are learned? Best practices and World Bank rural telecommunications policy. *Information Society*, 20(5), 345–356. DOI: 10.1080/01972240490507983. 28 , 45, 46, 48, 49, 50, 59, 65, 66

Courtright, C. (2005). Health information-seeking among Latino newcomers: an exploratory study. *Information Research-An International Electronic Journal*, 10(2). 36, 38, 45, 49, 50, 53, 60, 66

Cox, A. (2014). Turning to the practice approach in social informatics. In Fichman, P. and Rosenbaum H. (eds), *Social Informatics: Past, Present and Future*. Cambridge, UK. Cambridge Scholarly Publishers. 165–182. 24, 31, 39

Davenport, E. (2000). Social intelligence in the age of networks. *Journal Of Information Science*, 26(3), 145–152. DOI : 10.1177/016555150002600304. 29, 53, 61

Davenport, E. (2001). Knowledge management issues for online organisations: 'communities of practice' as an exploratory framework. *Journal Of Documentation*, 57(1), 61–75. DOI: 10.1108/EUM0000000007077. 29, 45, 46, 48, 49, 53, 60, 66

Davenport, E. (2005). Social informatics in practice: A guide for the perplexed. *Bulletin Of The American Society For Information Science and Technology*, 31(5), 17–20. DOI: 10.1002/bult.2005.1720310506. 21, 37, 53, 59, 65, 66

Davenport, E. (2008). Social informatics and socio-technical research - a view from the UK. *Journal Of Information Science*, 34(4), 519–530. DOI: 10.1177/0165551508091011. 13, 30, 38, 39

Davenport, E. and Horton, K. (2006). The production of services in the digital city: A social informatics inquiry. In: *Social Informatics: An Information Society for All? In Remembrance of Rob Kling*. pp. 233–242. DOI: 10.1007/978-0-387-37876-3_19. 30, 38, 46, 47, 48, 49, 50, 63, 64, 65, 66, 67, 68

Davenport, E. and Horton, K. (2007). Where and when was knowledge managed?. In: *Rethinking Knowledge Management* (p. 171). DOI: 10.1007/3-540-71011-6_7. 30, 38, 46, 47, 48, 49, 50, 54, 64, 65, 66

Davidson, E., and Lamb, R. (2000). Examining socio-technical networks in scientific academia/industry collaborations. *AMCIS 2000 Proceedings*, 202.

Day, R.E. (2007). Kling and the "critical": Social informatics and critical informatics. *Journal of the American Society for Information Science and Technology* 58 (4), 2007. DOI: 10.1002/asi.20546. 11, 30, 39, 47, 49

Doz, Y. L., Olk, P. M., and Smith, P. (2000) "Formation processes of R&D consortia: which path to take? Where does it lead?" *Strategic Management Journal*, 21(3) 239–266. DOI: 10.1002/(SICI)1097-0266(200003)21:3<239::AID-SMJ97>3.0.CO;2-K. 4, 5

Ekbia, H. R. and Kling, R. (2003). Power in knowledge management in late modern times. *Academy of Management Proceedings*, d1–d6. DOI: 10.5465/Ambpp.2003.13793113. 37, 48, 49, 53, 65

Ekbia, H. and Kling, R. (2005). Network organizations: Symmetric cooperation or multivalent negotiation?. *Information Society*, 21(3), 155–168. DOI: 10.1080/01972240490951881. 29, 35, 36, 45, 46, 48, 49, 50, 59, 60, 61, 65, 66, 67, 68

Elliott, M. S. and Kraemer, K. L. (2007). Introduction to the special issue on "The legacy of Rob Kling: Social informatics as a research discipline." *Information Society*, 23(4), 203–204. DOI: 10.1080/01972240701441523. 30, 47, 48, 49

Endo, K. and Abe, K. (2008). On the occasion of publication of the *Journal of Socio-Informatics*. *Journal of Socio-Informatics*, 1(1), 3–4. 12

Eschenfelder, K. (2014). Use regimes: A theoretical framework for social informatics research. In Fichman, P. and Rosenbaum H. (eds), *Social Informatics: Past, Present and Future*. Cambridge, UK. Cambridge Scholarly Publishers. 100–117. 24

Fichman, P. and Hara, N. (2014). *Global Wikipedia: International and Cross-Cultural Issues in Online Collaboration*. Rowman and Littlefield Publishers, Inc. 30

Fichman, P. and Rosenbaum, H. (2014). *Social Informatics: Past, Present and Future*. Cambridge Scholars Publishing. 1. 23, 30, 31

Fichman, P. and Sanfilippo, M. R. (2013). Multicultural issues in information and communications technology (ICT). In G. Marchionini (ed.) *Synthesis Lectures on Information Concepts, Retrieval, and Services*. Morgan & Claypool Publishers. 2

Fleischmann, K. (2014). Social informatics, human values, and ICT design. In Fichman, P. and Rosenbaum H. (eds), *Social Informatics: Past, Present and Future*. Cambridge, UK. Cambridge Scholarly Publishers. 73–88. 24, 31, 47

Frickel, S. and Gross, N. (2005). "A general theory of scientific/intellectual movements." *American Sociological Review*, 70(2), 204–233. DOI: 10.1177/000312240507000202. 7, 8

Godfrey-Smith, P. (2003). *Theory and Reality: An Introduction to the Philosophy of Science*. Chicago: University of Chicago Press. DOI: 10.7208/chicago/9780226300610.001.0001.

Goggins, S. P., Laffey, J., and Tsai, I. (2007, November). Cooperation and groupness: Community formation in small online collaborative groups. In *Proceedings of the 2007 International ACM Conference on Supporting Group Work* (pp. 207–216). ACM. DOI: 10.1145/1316624.1316654. 39

Goggins, S. P., Laffey, J., and Gallagher, M. (2011). Completely online group formation and development: small groups as socio-technical systems. *Information Technology and People*, 24(2), 104-133. DOI: 10.1108/09593841111137322. 23, 30, 38, 46, 47, 49, 50, 54, 63, 66, 67, 68

Hanks, S. H., Watson, C. J., Jansen, E., and Chandler, G. N. (1994). Tightening the life-cycle construct: A taxonomic study of growth stage configurations in high-technology organizations. *Entrepreneurship, Theory and Practice*, 18(2), 5–30. 4

Hara, N. and Kling, R. (2002). Communities of practice with and without information technology. *Proceedings of the 65th annual meeting of the American Society for Information Science and*

Technology, 39, 338–349. DOI: 10.1002/meet.1450390137. 28, 29, 36, 45, 46, 48, 50, 53, 59, 61, 62, 65, 67

Hara, N. and Rosenbaum, H. (2008). Revising the conceptualization of computerization movements. *Information Society*, 24(4), 229–245. DOI: 10.1080/01972240802191605. 38, 48, 49, 54, 64, 65

Hara, N., Shachaf, P., and Stoerger, S. (2009). Online communities of practice typology revisited. *Journal of Information Science*, 35(6), 740–757. DOI: 10.1177/0165551509342361. 23, 30, 63

Hara, N., Shachaf, P., and Hew, K. F. (2010). Cross-cultural analysis of the Wikipedia community. *Journal of the American Society for Information Science and Technology*, 61(10), 2097–2108. DOI: 10.1002/asi.21373. 23, 30, 47

Hite, J. M. and Hesterly, W. S. (2001). The evolution of firm networks: From emergence to early growth of the firm. *Strategic Management Journal* 22(3): 275–286. DOI: 10.1002/smj.156. 4, 5

Iacono, S. (1996). The demise of meaning-making and social agency as critical concepts in the rhetoric of an information age. *Information Society*, 12(4), 449. DOI: 10.1080/019722496129413. 20, 21, 26, 27, 42, 49, 52, 53, 56, 57, 58, 65, 66

Iacono, S., King, J., and Kraemer, K. L. (2003, September). Rob Kling: A remembrance. *Communications of AIS*. pp. 649–658. 22, 28, 29, 37, 45, 46, 48, 49, 53

Iacono, S. and Kling, R. (1988). Computer systems as institutions: Social dimensions of computing in organizations. In *Proceedings of the Ninth International Conference on Information Systems*, 11, pp. 30–12. 19, 20, 48

Kimbel, D. (1973). Computers and telecommunications; economic, technical and organisational issues. OECD Informatics Studies, #3.

King, J., Iacono, S., and Grudin, J. (2007). Going critical: Perspective and proportion in the epistemology of Rob Kling. *Information Society*, 23(4), 251–262. DOI: 10.1080/01972240701444170. 30, 39, 46, 47, 48, 49, 63, 64, 66

Kling, R. (1994). Reading "all about" computerization: How genre conventions shape non-fiction social analysis. *Information Society*, 10(3), 147–172. DOI: 10.1080/01972243.1994.9960166. 21, 26, 27, 34, 42, 44, 49, 52

Kling, R. (1996). *Computerization and Controversy: Value Conflicts and Social Choices*. Edited by Rob Kling. San Diego : Academic Press, c1996. DOI: 10.1016/B978-0-12-415040-9.50089-0. 26, 27, 34, 42, 43, 44, 48, 49, 52, 56, 57, 58, 65, 66

Kling, R. (1997). The Internet for sociologists. *Rob Kling Center for Social Informatics Working Papers Series*, WP-97-02. Other versions: Kling, R. (1997). The Internet for sociologists. *Contemporary Sociology-a Journal of Reviews*, 26(4), 434–444. DOI: 10.2307/2655084. 21, 26, 43, 44, 50, 52

Kling, R. (1998). A brief introduction to social informatics. *Canadian Journal of Information and Library Science - Revue Canadienne des Sciences de l'Information et de Bibliotheconomie*, 23(1-2), 50–85. x, 4, 21, 26, 27, 42, 43, 48, 50, 52, 53, 56, 57, 58, 65, 66, 67

Kling, R. (1999). Can the "next generation Internet" effectively support "ordinary citizens"? *Information Society*, 15(1), 57–63. DOI: 10.1080/019722499128673. 16, 21, 26, 27, 42, 43, 44, 48, 50, 52, 56, 57, 58, 65, 66, 67

Kling, R. (1999). What is social informatics and why does it matter? *D-Lib Magazine*. http://www.dlib.org/dlib/january99/kling/01kling.html (Retrieved March 23, 2013). DOI: 10.1080/01972240701441556. 42, 43, 44, 48, 49, 56, 57

Kling, R. (2000a). Learning about information technologies and social change: The contribution of social informatics. *Information Society*, 16(3), 217–232. DOI: 10.1080/01972240050133661. 21, 22, 27, 28, 29, 36, 37, 45, 46, 48, 49, 50, 53, 58, 59, 61, 66, 67, 74

Kling, R. (2000b). Social informatics: A new perspective on social research about information and communication technologies. *Prometheus*, 18(3), 245–264. DOI: 10.1080/713692067. 21, 22, 27, 28, 36, 46, 48, 50, 53, 58, 59, 60, 61, 65, 66, 67

Kling, R. (2001). The Internet and the strategic reconfiguration of libraries. *Library Administration and Management*, 15(3), 16–23. 28, 46, 50, 53, 58, 59, 60, 61, 65, 66, 67

Kling, R. (2003a). Critical professional education about information and communications technologies and social life. *Information Technology and People*, 16(4), 394–418. DOI: 10.1108/09593840310509635. 28

Kling, R. (2003b). Social informatics. In A. Kent, H. Lancour, W. Z. Nasri and J. E. Daily (Eds.), *Encyclopedia of Library and Information Science*. New York: Marcel Dekker, Inc. 16, 28, 37, 45, 46, 48, 49, 50, 53, 58, 59, 60, 65, 66, 67

Kling, R. and Callahan, E. (2003). Electronic journals, the Internet, and scholarly communication. *Annual Review Of Information Science and Technology*, 37(1), 127–177. DOI: 10.1002/aris.1440370105. 23, 28, 37, 46, 50, 53, 59, 65, 67

Kling, R. and Courtright, C. (2003). Group behavior and learning in electronic forums: A socio-technical approach. *Information Society*, 19(3), 221. DOI: /10.1080/01972240309465. 22, 28, 45, 46, 49, 50, 53, 60, 65, 66

Kling, R., Crawford, H., Rosenbaum, H., Sawyer, S., and Weisband, S. (2000). Learning from social informatics: Information and communication technologies in human contexts. *Report to the National Science Foundation.*

Kling, R. and Hara, N. (2004). Informatics and distributed learning, In A. DiStefano, K. Rudestam, R. Silverman, and S. Taira (Eds.), *Encyclopedia of Distributed Learning* (pp. 225–227). Thousand Oaks, CA: Sage Publications. DOI: 10.4135/9781412950596.n80. 21, 28, 29, 46, 48, 49, 53, 59, 60, 65, 66

Kling, R. and Iacono, S. (1984a). Computing as an occasion for social control. *Journal Of Social Issues*, 4077–96. http://dx.doi.org/10.1111/j.1540-4560.1984.tb00193.x. 19, 33, 34, 41, 48, 51, 55, 56, 65

Kling, R. and Iacono, S. (1984b). The control of information systems developments after implementation. *Communications Of The ACM*, 27(12), 1218–1226. DOI: 10.1145/2135.358307. 19, 25, 33, 34, 41, 48, 51, 55, 56, 65

Kling, R. and Iacono, S. (1988). The mobilization of support for computerization: The role of computerization movements. *Social Problems*, (3), 226. DOI: 10.2307/800620. 19, 26, 33, 34, 41, 42, 49, 51, 55, 56, 65

Kling, R. and Iacono, S. (1989). The institutional character of computerized information systems. *Information Technology and People*, 5(1), 7. DOI: 10.1108/eum0000000003526. 19, 26, 33, 34, 41, 48, 49, 51, 55, 56, 65, 66

Kling, R. and Iacono, S. (2001). Computerizaton movements: The rise of the Internet and distant forms of work. In J. Yates and J. V. Maanan (Eds.), *Information Technology and Organizational Transformation: History, Rhetoric, and Practice* (pp. 93–136). Thousand Oakes, CA: Sage Publications. DOI: 10.4135/9781452231266. 22, 28, 37, 45, 49, 53, 59, 61, 65, 67

Kling, R. and Lamb, R. (1996). Bits of cities: Utopian visions and social power in placed-based and electronic communities. *Rob Kling Center for Social Informatics Working Papers Series*, WP-96-02. Other versions: Kling, R., and Lamb, R. (1998). Morceaux de villes. Comment les visions utopiques structurent le pouvoir social dans l'espace physique et dans le cyberespace. In E. Eveno (Ed.), *Utopies Urbaines*. Presses Universitaires du Mirail. 21, 26, 43, 44, 49, 50, 52, 56, 57, 58, 65, 66, 67

Kling, R. and Lamb, R. (1999). IT and organizational change in digital economies. *Computers and Society*, 29(3), 17. DOI: 10.1145/572183.572189. 21, 26, 34, 43, 44, 48, 49, 50, 52, 56, 57, 58, 66, 67

Kling, R. and McKim, G. W. (2000). Not just a matter of time: field differences and the shaping of electronic media in supporting scientific communication. *Journal Of The American Society For In-*

formation Science, 51(14), 1306–1320. DOI: 10.1002/1097-4571(2000)9999:9999<::AID-ASI1047>3.0.CO;2-T. 28, 29, 36, 45, 46, 48, 50, 53, 59, 66

Kling, R., McKim, G., and King, A. (2003). A bit more to it: Scholarly communication forums as socio-technical interaction networks. *Journal Of The American Society For Information Science And Technology*, 54(1), 47–67. DOI: 10.1002/asi.10154. 22, 28, 36, 37, 45, 46, 49, 50, 53, 58, 59, 60, 61, 62, 65, 66, 67

Kling, R., Rosenbaum, H., and Hert, C. (1998). Social informatics in information science: An introduction. *Journal of the American Society for Information Science*, 49(12), 1047–1052. DOI: 10.1002/(SICI)1097-4571(1998)49:12<1047::AID-ASI1>3.3.CO;2-O. 26, 42, 43, 44, 49, 50

Kling, R., Rosenbaum, H., and Sawyer, S. (2005). *Understanding and Communicating Social Informatics: A Framework for Studying and Teaching the Human Contexts of Information and Communication Technologies*. Rob Kling, Howard Rosenbaum, Steve Sawyer. Medford, N.J. : Information Today, Inc., 2005. 7, 15, 16, 21, 22, 28, 29, 45, 48, 49, 53, 58, 59, 60, 61, 62, 65, 66, 67

Kling, R., Rosenbaum, H., Sawyer, S, Weisband, S, and Crawford, H. (2001). Information technologies in human contexts: Learning from organizational and social informatics. *Report to the National Foundation on the Workshop on Social Informatics* (1997).

Kling, R. and Star, L. (1997). Human-centered systems in the perspective of organizational and social informatics (chapter 5). In T. Huang and J. Flanigan (Eds.), *Human Centered Systems, for the National Science Foundation*. 21, 26, 27, 34, 35, 42, 43, 44, 48, 49, 50, 52, 53, 56, 57, 58, 65, 66, 67

Kling, R. and Tillquist, T. (1998). Conceiving IT-enabled organizational change. *Rob Kling Center for Social Informatics Working Papers Series*, WP-98-02. 26, 34, 42, 43, 44, 48, 49, 50, 52, 56, 57, 65, 66

Kolin K.K. (1994). Social informatics - Scientific basis of postindustrial society. *Social Informatics*, 94, 4–23. 11

Kolin, K. (2011). Social Informatics Today and Tomorrow: Status, Problems and Prospects of Development of Complex Lines in the Field of Science and Education. Triple C: Cognition, Communication, Co-operaiton. 460–465. http://www.triple-c.at. 11

Kuhn, T. S. (1962). *The Structure of Scientific Revolutions*. Chicago; London: The University of Chicago Press. DOI: 10.1002/1520-6696(196607)2:3<274::AID-JHBS2300020312>3.0.CO;2-7.

Kuhn, T. S. (1969). Second thoughts on paradigms. In T. S. Kuhn, *The Structure of Scientific Revolutions*, Second Edition. Chicago; London: The University of Chicago Press, c1970.

Kumon, S. (2008). An infosocionomist's view. *Journal of Socio-Informatics*, 1(1), 6–20.

Kurosu, T. (2010). In search of a paradigm of socio-informatics: On socio-informatics and social informatics. *Journal of Socio-Informatics* Vol. 3 No. 1, 69–81. 12, 13

Lamb, R. (1996). Informational imperatives and socially mediated relationships. *Information Society*, 12(1), 17. DOI: 10.1080/019722496129684. 2, 21, 34, 35, 42, 43, 44, 48, 49, 50, 52, 56, 57, 66

Lamb, R. (2003). Memorial: The social construction of Rob Kling. *Information Society*, 19(3), 195. DOI: 10.1080/01972240309463. 22, 28, 36, 37, 45, 49, 50

Lamb, R. (2005). Modeling the social actor. *North American Association for Computational Social and Organizational Systems (NAACSOS)*, Notre Dame, Indiana. 49

Lamb, R. and Davidson, E. (2005). Information and communication technology challenges to scientific professional identity. *Information Society*, 21(1), 1–24. DOI: 10.1080/01972240590895883. 28, 35, 36, 37, 45, 46, 48, 50, 59, 61, 62, 65, 67, 68

Lamb, R., King, J., and Kling, R. (2003). Informational environments: Organizational contexts of onlineinformation Use. *Journal Of The American Society For Information Science And Technology*, 54(2), 97–114. DOI: http://dx.doi.org/10.1002/asi.10182. 37, 45, 46, 48, 49, 50, 53, 59, 60, 65, 66, 67

Lamb, R. and Kling, R. (2003). Reconceptualizing users as social actors in information systems research. *MIS Quarterly*, 27(2), 197–235. 28, 29, 36, 37, 45, 46, 48, 50, 53, 59, 60, 61, 65, 66, 67

Lamb, R. and Sawyer, S. (2005). On extending social informatics from a rich legacy of networks and conceptual resources. *Information Technology and People*, 18(1), 9–20. DOI: 10.1108/09593840510584595. 22, 27, 28, 29, 36, 37, 38, 45, 49, 59, 60, 61, 62, 65, 66, 67

Le Roux, C. J. B. (2009). Social and community informatics past, present and future: An historic overview. *10th Annual DIS Conference* 10–11 September.

Lessard, L. (2014). Reframing the socio-technical problem: A way forward for social-informatics. In Fichman, P. and Rosenbaum H. (eds), *Social Informatics: Past, Present and Future*. Cambridge, UK. Cambridge Scholarly Publishers. 136–151. 23, 30, 31, 39

Maldonado, E. A., Maitland, C. F., and Tapia, A. H. (2010). Collaborative systems development in disaster relief: The impact of multi-level governance. *Information Systems Frontiers*, 12(1), 9. DOI: 10.1007/s10796-009-9166-z. 38, 39, 46, 47, 48, 49, 50, 54, 63, 64, 65, 66

Mansell, R. (2005). Social informatics and the political economy of communications. *Information Technology and People*, 18(1), 21–25. DOI: 10.1108/09593840510584603. 22, 29, 35, 36, 45, 49, 50, 59, 60, 65, 66, 67

Meyer, E. T. (2006). Socio-technical interaction networks: A discussion of the strengths, weaknesses and future of Kling's STIN model. In *Social Informatics: An Information Society for All? In Remembrance of Rob Kling* (pp. 37–48). Springer US. DOI: 10.1007/978-0-387-37876-3_3. 38, 63

Meyer, D.S. and Rohlinger, D.A. (2012). Big books and social movements: A myth of ideas and social change. *Social Problems*, 59(1), 136–153. DOI: 10.1525/sp.2012.59.1.136. 8

Meyer, E. (2014). Examining the hyphen: The value of social informatics for research and teaching. In Fichman, P. and Rosenbaum H. (eds), *Social Informatics: Past, Present and Future*. Cambridge, UK. Cambridge. 56–71. 23, 31, 75

Meyer, E. T. and Kling, R. (2002). Leveling the playing field, or expanding the bleachers? Socio-technical interaction networks and arXiv.org. *Rob Kling Center for Social Informatics Working Papers Series*, WP-02-10. 27, 37, 45, 50, 53, 59, 60, 61, 65, 66, 67, 68

Ngamassi, L., Zhao, K., Maldonado, E., Maitland, C., and Tapia, A. H. (2011). Humanitarian information exchange network: why do international humanitarian organisations collaborate?. *International Journal Of Society Systems Science*, 3(4), 362. DOI: 10.1504/IJSSS.2011.043213.

Niblett, G.B.F. (1971). Informatics studies: No 2: Digital information and the privacy problem. *Organization for Economic Development and Cooperation Informatics Studies*, #2.

Nishigaki, T. and Takenouchi, T. (2009). The informatic turn-who observes the "infosphere"? *Journal of Socio-Informatics*, 2(1), 81–90. 13

Oltmann, S. M., Rosenbaum, H., and Hara, N. (2006). Digital access to government information: To what extent are agencies in compliance with EFOIA?. *Proceedings Of The American Society For Information Science And Technology*, 43(1), 1. DOI: 10.1002/meet.14504301190. 30, 39, 46, 48, 50, 54, 63, 64, 65, 66, 68

Orlikowski, W. J. and Iacono, C. (2008). Research commentary : desperately seeking the 'IT' in IT research : a call to theorizing the IT artifact. In, *Information Systems Infrastructure* (pp. 280–297). DOI: 10.1287/isre.12.2.121.9700. 39, 47, 49, 62, 63, 67

Parsons, T. (1966). *Societies: Evolutionary and Comparative Perspectives*. New Jersey: Prentice-Hall. 5

Racherla, P. and Mandviwalla, M. (2013). Moving from access to use of the information infrastructure: a multilevel socio-technical framework. *Information Systems Research*, (3), 709. DOI: 10.1287/isre.2013.0477. 24, 39

Ring, PS. and Van de Ven, AH. 1994. Developmental processes of cooperative interorganizational relationships. *Academy of Management Review* 19(1): 90–118. DOI: 10.5465/ AMR.1994.9410122009. 4, 5

Robbin, A. (2007). Rob Kling in search of one good theory. *Information Society*, 23(4), 235–250. DOI: 10.1080/01972240701444154. 39, 46, 49

Robbin, A. and Day, R. (2006). On Rob Kling: The theoretical, the methodological, and the critical. In: *Social Informatics: An Information Society for All? In rememberance of Rob Kling.* Pp. 25–36. DOI: 10.1007/978-0-387-37876-3_2. 10, 30, 39, 46, 47, 48, 49, 50, 63, 65, 66

Robbin, A., Lamb, R., King, J. L., Berleur, J. (2006). Social informatics: An information society for all? In remembrance of Rob Kling. *IFIP International Federation for Information Processing*, 223/2206, 17–21. DOI: 10.1007/978-0-387-37876-3_1. 38, 46, 47, 48, 49, 50, 63, 64, 65, 66, 67

Roggen, I. (2005). Personal communication, email, October 17. 10, 15

Roggen, I. (1998). Specialization course in web sociology and social Informatics http://folk.uio.no/ iroggen/WEBsociologyINFOeng.html. 10

Rosenbaum, H. (2009). Social informatics. *Encyclopedia of Library and Information Science.* New York, New York: Marcel Dekker, Inc., 2656–2661. 16

Rosenbaum, H. (2014). The past: Brief comments on the history of social informatics. In Fichman, P. and Rosenbaum H. (eds), *Social Informatics: Past, Present and Future.* Cambridge, UK. Cambridge Scholarly Publishers. 2–28. 16

Rosenbaum, H. and Shachaf, P. (2010). A structuration approach to online communities of practice: The case of Q&A communities. *Journal Of The American Society For Information Science And Technology*, 61(9), 1933–1944. DOI: 10.1002/asi.21340. 23, 30, 39, 47, 49, 50, 54, 62, 63, 64, 65, 66

Sanfilippo, M. and Fichman, P. (2014). The evolution of social informatics research (1984-2013): Challenges and opportunities. In Fichman, P. and Rosenbaum H. (eds), *Social Informatics: Past, Present and Future.* Cambridge, UK. Cambridge Scholarly Publishers. 29–55. 7, 19, 24, 30, 31, 47, 63, 64

Sawyer, S. (2005). Social informatics: Overview, principles and opportunities. *Bulletin Of The American Society For Information Science and Technology*, 31(5), 9–12. DOI: 10.1002/ bult.2005.1720310504. 29, 45, 46, 48, 49, 53, 59, 60, 61, 65, 66, 67

Sawyer, S. and Eschenfelder, K. (2002). Social informatics: perspectives, examples, and trends. *Annual Review Of Information Science And Technology*, Volume 36, 427–465. DOI: 10.1002/ aris.1440360111. 22, 28, 29, 37, 45, 48, 49, 53, 59, 60, 61, 65, 66, 67

Sawyer, S. and Hartswood, M. (2014). Advancing social informatics. In Fichman, P. and Rosenbaum H. (eds), *Social Informatics: Past, Present and Future*. Cambridge, UK. Cambridge Scholarly Publishers. 195–220. 23, 24, 31

Sawyer, S. and Rosenbaum, H. (2000). Social informatics in the information sciences: current activities and emerging directions. *Informing Science*, 3(2), 89–96. 27, 28, 29, 37, 45, 50, 58, 59, 60, 61, 65, 66, 67

Sawyer, S. and Tapia, A. (2005). The socio-technical nature of mobile computing work: Evidence from a study of policing in the United States. *International Journal Of Technology And Human Interaction*, 1(3), 1. DOI: 10.4018/jthi.2005070101. 28, 36, 45, 46, 48, 53, 59, 65

Sawyer, S. and Tapia, A. (2006). Always articulating: Theorizing on mobile and wireless technologies. *Information Society*, 22(5), 311–323. DOI: 10.1080/01972240600904258. 30, 39, 49, 54, 63, 64, 65, 67

Sawyer, S. and Tapia, A. (2007). From findings to theories: Institutionalizing social informatics. *Information Society*, 23(4), 263–275. DOI: 10.1080/01972240701444196. 15, 16, 39, 47, 48

Sawyer, S. and Tyworth, M. (2006). Social informatics: Principles, theory, and practice. In, *Social Informatics: An Information Society for all? In Remembrance of Rob Kling* (p. 49). DOI: 10.1007/978-0-387-37876-3_4. 30, 38, 39, 46, 47, 49, 50, 54, 63, 64, 66, 67

School of Informatics. Edinburgh University. (2012). Vision. Overview. http://www.ed.ac.uk/informatics/about/welcome. 14

Shachaf, P. (2003). Nationwide consortia life cycle. *LIBRI: International Journal of Libraries and Information Services*, 53(2), 94+102. DOI: 10.1515/LIBR.2003.94. 4

Shachaf, P. and Hara, N. 2005. Team effectiveness in virtual environments: An ecological approach. In P. Ferris and S. Godar (Eds.), *Teaching and Learning with Virtual Teams* pp. 83+108. Hershey, PA: Idea Group Publishing, Inc. DOI: 10.4018/978-1-59140-708-9.ch004. 4

Shachaf, P. (2008). Cultural diversity and information and communication technology impacts on global virtual teams: An exploratory study. *Information and Management*, 45(2), 131-142. DOI: 10.1016/j.im.2007.12.003. 23, 47, 63, 64

Shachaf, P. and Hara, N. (2007). Behavioral complexity theory of media selection: a proposed theory for global virtual teams. *Journal of Information Science*, 33(1), 63–75. DOI: 10.1177/0165551506068145. 23, 30, 31, 39, 47, 54, 63, 64, 65, 66, 68

Shachaf, P., Oltmann, S. M., and Horowitz, S. M. (2008). Service equality in virtual reference. *Journal of the American Society for Information Science and Technology*, 59(4), 535–550. DOI: 10.1002/asi.20757. 64

Shachaf, P., and Rosenbaum, H. (2009). Online social reference: A research agenda through a STIN framework. *iConference 2009*. http://hdl.handle.net/2142/15209. 38, 63

Shachaf, P. (2010). Social reference: Toward a unifying theory. *Library and Information Science Research*, 32(1), 66-76. DOI: 10.1016/j.lisr.2009.07.009. 23

Shin, Y. and Shin, D. (2012). Community informatics and the new urbanism: incorporating information and communication technologies into planning integrated urban communities. *Journal Of Urban Technology*, 19(1), 23–42. DOI: 10.1080/10630732.2012.626698. 30, 64

Simpson, G. (2014). Projects and objects: Points of contact between textual studies and socio-technical investigations. In Fichman, P. and Rosenbaum H. (eds), *Social Informatics: Past, Present and Future*. Cambridge, UK. Cambridge Scholarly Publishers. 152–164. 39

Singh, M. P. (2013). Norms as a basis for governing socio-technical systems. *ACM Transactions On Intelligent Systems And Technology*, 5(1). DOI: 10.1145/2542182.2542203. 39, 63

Social Informatics Cluster. School of Informatics. Edinburgh University. (2012). Social Informatics Cluster. https://wiki.inf.ed.ac.uk/Main/SIC. 14

Stillman, L. and Linger, H. (2009). Community informatics and information systems: Can they be better connected?. *Information Society*, 25(4), 255–264. DOI: 10.1080/01972240903028706. 24, 30, 63

Sundstrom, E., DeMuese, KP., and Futrell D. (1990). Work teams: Applications and effectiveness. *The American Psychologist* 45(2): 120–133. DOI: 10.1037/0003-066X.45.2.120. 4

Tapia, A. H., Kvasny, L., and Ortiz, J. A. (2011). A critical discourse analysis of three U.S. municipal wireless network initiatives for enhancing social inclusion. *Telematics and Informatics*, 28(3), 215–226. DOI: 10.1016/j.tele.2010.07.002. , 54

Tapia, A. and Maitland, C. (2009). Wireless devices for humanitarian data collection. *Information, Communication and Society*,12(4), 584–604. DOI: 10.1080/13691180902857637. 30, 39, 46, 47, 48, 49, 50, 54, 63, 64, 65, 67, 68

The Faculty of Social Sciences, University of Ljubljana, Slovenia. *Social Informatics*. 2007. http://www.social-informatics.org/index.php?fl=0&p1=181&p2=5&p3=&id=197 (accessed July 2013). 10

Tuckman, BW. (1965). Developmental sequences in small groups. *Psychological Bulletin* 63: 384-399. DOI: 10.1037/h0022100.

Tuckman, BW. and Jensen, MAC. (1977). Stages of small group development revisited. *Group and Organization Studies* 2(4): 419–427. DOI: 10.1177/105960117700200404.

UNESCO. Institute for Information Technologies in Education (nd). 2nd International Congress on Education and Informatics. http://iite.unesco.org/publications/3214575/. 11

Ursul, A.D. (1989). On the shaping of social informatics. *International Forum on Information and Documentation*, 14(4): 10–18. 10, 11, 73

Vehovar. V. (2006). Social informatics: An emerging discipline? In In Berleur, J., Nurminen, M.I. and Impagliazzo, J. (eds). *Social Informatics: An Information Society for All? Remembrance of Rob Kling: Proceedings of the Seventh International Conference on Human Choice and Computers* (HCC7), IFIP TC 9, Maribor, Slovenia, September 21–23, 73–85. DOI: 10.1007/978-0-387-37876-3_6. 10

Vehovar, V. (2013a). History. Social Informatics.org University of Ljubljana, Faculty of Social Sciences. http://www.social-informatics.org/c/133/History?preid=197. 10

Vehovar, V. (2013b). Study Programs. Social Informatics.org University of Ljubljana, Faculty of Social Sciences http://www.social-informatics.org/index.php?fl=2&p1=181&p2=151&lact=3&bid=5. 10, 75

Wade, P. (2014). Race, ethnicity, and technologies of belonging. *Science, Technology and Human Values*, 39(4), 587–596. DOI: 10.1177/0162243913516807. 30, 62, 63

Walker, S., and Creanor, L. (2009). The STIN in the tale: a socio-technical interaction perspective on networked learning. *Journal of Educational Technology and Society*, 12(4), 305–316. 63

Wicker, A. W. (1979). *An Introduction to Ecological Psychology*. Belmont, CA: Wadsworth, Inc, 1979.

Wolpert, L., Beddington, R., Brockes, J., Jessell, T., Lawrence, P., and Meyerowitz, E. 1(998). Principles of development. *Current Biology Ltd London*. 5

Wood-Harper, T. and Wood, B. (2005). Multiview as social informatics in action: past, present and future. *Information Technology and People*, 18(1), 26–32. DOI: 10.1108/09593840510585918. 22, 37, 45, 49, 50, 53, 59, 60, 65, 66

Yoshida, T. (2008). Supertemporal and temporal-constrained tharacters of socioinformatics. *Journal of Socio-Informatics*, 1(1), 37–45. 12

Author Biographies

Pnina Fichman is an Associate Professor in the School of Informatics and Computing, the Director of the Rob Kling Center of Social Informatics, and the Chair of the Department of Information and Library Science at Indiana University, Bloomington. Her research in social informatics focuses on the relationships between information technologies and cultural diversity, and the consequences and impacts of this interaction on group process and outcomes. She studies processes and outcomes of crowds, online communities, virtual teams, and information intermediation. In addition, her research addresses motivation for, perception of, and reaction to online deviant behaviors, such as trolling and discrimination. In addition to her five co-edited/authored books, her publications appeared for example in: *Information and Management*, *Journal of the American Society for Information Science and Technology*, and *Journal of Information Science*. She earned her Ph.D. from the School of Information and Library Science, University of North Carolina, Chapel Hill in 2003.

Madelyn Sanfilippo is a doctoral candidate in Information Science at Indiana University, Bloomington's School of Informatics and Computing. Madelyn is interested in the relationships between politics and information. Her work specifically addresses social and political issues surrounding information and information technology access; she considers the interaction between information policy and information technology as it impacts information access, from a social informatics perspective, in her dissertation.

Howard Rosenbaum is Professor of Information Science in the Department of Information and Library Science and Associate Dean for Graduate Studies in the School of Informatics and Computing at Indiana University. He has been at Indiana University since 1993 where he has been teaching courses in social informatics, digital entrepreneurship, information science, and intellectual freedom. He has won many awards for his innovative uses of technology in education, including the 2011 Thomson Reuters Outstanding Information Science Teacher Award. His research focuses on social informatics, e-business, and online communities, and he has published in a variety of information science journals and presented at ASIS&T, iConferences, and elsewhere. In 2005, he published "Information Technologies in Human Contexts: Learning from Organizational and Social Informatics" with Steve Sawyer and the late Rob Kling. With Pnina Fichman, he published an edited collection, "Social Informatics: Past, Present, and Future," in 2014. He has been involved in social informatics since 1997 and works with collaborators to raise the profile of SI in the information sciences.